"PASSION"

Toolset for Initiative Fatigue. Permanently shifting mental blocks of coaches leaders and learning students.

Image: Colin Behrens lightbulb

© 2018 Rachael Orchard. All rights reserved. Without the explicit authorization of the editor, none of the author's ideas can be reproduced.

TM PASSION Toolset is a pending trademark tool of MyPocketCoach

PASSION Toolset Publishing

The ISBN number is 978-1-9993531-0-0

Printed in the United Kingdom

Credit for cover design is Colin Behrens, Lightbulb. All images are taken from www.Pixabay.com and their artists are listed in the back pages of this book.

Dedication

To my children whom I am so proud of. You will always be my guiding lights, my reason to want to continue to be the best mother and me for you; always questioning how I can listen more, learn more and be more

Preface

I designed PASSION Toolset from a frustration I had over these last six years of my coaching experience. I felt there was a lack of consistency when it came to changing behaviour through coaching and training delivery.

The PASSION toolset I then designed encapsulates all the principles you could ever wish to learn about coaching/ philosophy/ behavioural change. But more importantly, the toolset acts as a daily guide or even a diagnostic tool such as one you might find on a car dashboard. Once you understand the meaning of each letter, then as daily life occurs, you can refer back to the toolset so as to quickly diagnose where you may have an emotional or mental block to a situation.

What it provides:

- ✓ a successful way of encorporating and smashing goals in your daily life
- ✓ a new daily lens for understanding how we experience the world
- ✓ gives you themes to calibrate with
- ✓ freedom within a frame - a feeling context
- ✓ you just need the ideas you don't need the answers
- ✓ the value of words and how having a new tool i.e. PASSION can frame words in a new way, "which is more powerful than the atomic bomb" (George Raveling)

The context for this book is based on my fledgling interest in stoicism. You may have heard this related to the teachings of Marcus Aurelius, the Roman Emperor and more recently Ryan Holiday an American author. The main tenet behind it is - perception/ action/ willpower. Once you have read my definitions of the PASSION tools at the beginning of each chapter, you will understand that the tools have a similar theme to the one this follows.

For example, we have a choice over how we choose to interpret every situation. That there is a big emphasis on 'just' moving forward with small actions. And when things are out of our control, it sometimes takes pure willpower to make the best of it, maybe even something beyond willpower. You could put this down to high performance habits, wisdom or even the more recently over-used word of resilience.

This is also highlighted through the work of Robert Greene, the mentor of Ryan Holiday. The two pinnacle ideas he was recently discussing were:

1/ Being receptive to the negative things - these hold the greatest learnings for us.

2/ Character is our biggest asset and you cannot hide yours, but you can work on it and the 'patterns' as Robert says that are hidden.

I would like you to use PASSION to become more aware of YOUR character and decide what are the patterns you want to be responsible for. After you have finished the book, I would love to know what it might have added to your process of navigating life, how you perform and your fulfilment from doing so.

Please post any thoughts or feedback in the PASSION community www.facebook.com/Passiontoolset or email me at rachael@mypocketcoach.co.uk

Rachael Orchard

Cambridgeshire, United Kingdom

November 2018

Introduction

The PASSION toolset is my acronym for the seven Drivers of Personal Development. At the beginning of each chapter I will give a short explanation of what that particular letter in PASSION stands for. I then use a series of sections including storytelling, discovery tools and quotes to illustrate how you can easily integrate PASSION into your life. Many of my students say that after a very short space of time they begin to have a natural knowing where their blocks are and which of the tools they can use effectively to cause a permanent shift in the way they deal with that situation. A lot of my coaching is based around ontology, an ability to understand who you are being in a given situation.

I have had many personal triumphs from utilising the toolset daily and I hope the book will demonstrate this with some of the storytelling and directional questions I use. Moving forward, new challenges and mental blocks still require me to access PASSION because continuous improvement will always create the need to develop yourself. There is no "I've got there, so I'm writing a book." I think all Personal Development authors are just progressing on to the next level, of which there are endless steps to summit if you choose to. This attitude could be very useful if used in the context of mental health - people are not 'just depressed' or 'not depressed', there are always gradients. In fact I see learning as spherical not linear. The best way to explain this is to liken it to a multi-dimensional approach where it can be accessed in many different ways and progress is not always ahead of you it can be behind you, to the side of you etc and it is not static, i.e you don't achieve it once, it is continual.

For your ease of use, I have added notes lines to each page for ways of capturing your continuing professional development, as thoughts occur to you about your mental blocks as you read PASSION.

Directions for Book:

Each chapter has the following sub-headings for each PASSION tool:

1/ A Definition
2/ Why this tool is beneficial in your life
3/ My journey with each tool before and after
4/ When you know it's present
5/ When you know it's not present
6/ Daily calibration tool
7/ What changes will you make after reading this chapter

How to use:

1/ Read the 'definition' and 'benefits' of the tool.

2/ Begin to understand what it's like to live the tool through my story of the 'journey' before and after using each tool in PASSION.

3/ Start to make notes on how it relates to your life and then begin to notice if you have more ticks in the 'when you know it's present' as opposed to 'when you know it's not present' sections.

4/ Practice the tool daily using the 'daily calibration' exercise and set your 'changes' you wish to make at the end of each chapter.

Measurement:

The final piece of the toolset is setting a goal for yourself, or else what is the point of personal development? I ask you to tune into your radio frequency of "CHANNEL WBB" and you will find a page for each of these goal setting tools at the beginning of the book after the contents page.

WHO - who you are at your core and what excites you

BEHAVIOUR - daily actioning a higher performing behaviour

BELIEF - minimising any limiting belief

I would like you to set your goal as you see fit-either when you start the book or as you are reading the book; or even change the goal as you go. The point is to make reading PASSION as effective as possible and to do so you have to be noticing daily what goal you've set for yourself and what behaviour and belief is not helping or helping you achieve this. Then using each PASSION tool you can diagnose any blocks, i.e. you begin to see through reading the chapters, that one tool is missing in your life more than the others and that is where you can do some work.

Book Main Takeaway:

I designed the book to provide you a Toolset which enables continuous development in any area you pick and that it is so easy to use you forget you're doing the work. It is also a self-care tool, a way of armour-plating your mind, so you can become even more indestructible to what life has to throw at you. But it will take daily work and practicing the toolset to cause a sustainable ongoing permanent shift in your life.

Resources:

If you've enjoyed reading PASSION and would like to continue using the PASSION Toolset in your life, please email Rachael@mypocketcoach.co.uk and I can add you to my PASSION Toolset community.

You will have the option of joining a monthly group where you will receive an exclusive Workshop Webinar with me on a more detailed insight into the Tools used. Plus access to daily automated "nudges", weekly accountability calls and a private online group.

There is also an option for me to do a "Fireside chat" personal appearance at your company and share how the Toolset provides me a barometer and daily measure to improve my performance and that of my clients.

Acknowledgments:

To my parents and family who have always supported me. To my closest friends Sophie, Lisa and personal trainer Mark; you have been my rocks this past decade. To my accountability buddy of four years, Roberta, your listening has been crucial. And to all the mentors I have had in the past. Special thanks to my current mentor, Kathy, you are awesome, you inspire me, and without your belief in me I wouldn't have written this book.

Special acknowledgment:

All of the wonderful pictures in this book are from the amazingly talented photographers who publish their work on www.pixabay.com. They are free for commercial use and is a place they can practice and market their work in a public arena. I have contacted some of the artists like the one for my front cover and they are very happy their work is being used for public consumption in a way that is making a difference. I would still ask you please make an effort to stop by and support their work. After all, pictures paint a thousand words and more importantly, demonstrate the 'feelings' behind the quotes, which as you may have discovered, when you feel it, you understand it.

Table of Contents

Dedication	3
Preface	5
Introduction	7
Table of contents	11

Chapters

1 Power	15
2 Authenticity	39
3 Saying what you are going to do	61
4 Sticking to what you say	73
5 Index	87
6 Obstacles	99
7 Navigation	115
Bibliography	127
Photographers	138
About the Author page	140

WHO

List here what really excites you and what goal you could set around this area... (Remember to make it specific, measurable, achievable, realistic, timed)

BEHAVIOUR

List here a daily 10 minute action which starts to achieve higher performing behaviour in the area of your goal. Plus start being really honest about low performing behaviours i.e. if you are easily distracted, say I'm unfocused and want to be more disciplined. If you're overweight, say I'm fat and want to lose weight. No room for pussy footing around in this section. If we can't claim it we are not able to move past it...

LIMITING BELIEF

List here any limiting beliefs you start to notice around your new goal...

Passion

Chapter 1

POWER

Understanding you have the magic wand

POWER - Understanding you have the magic wand

Definition:

Begin to understand where you are giving and taking energy to/ from a situation. A master gives of themselves, is humble and remains un-triggered by situations. Understand you ARE the environment and to be a master and a role model, always demand clarity and seek to positively impact everyone and everything. Learning to see yourself as a self-generating battery and train yourself to see what saps the energy - consistently ask of yourself - how will that make me feel if I do this?

"*If you pursue excellence (not money) it's like a beacon people see it - and then the markets move the money to the excellence.*" Greg Glassman, founder CrossFit talking to Lewis Howes

"I was chasing my tail, doing every job possible in acting, then was fortuitous to meet Johnny Depp and he just calmly said, What's the rush?" Wilmer Valderrama, American Actor

"Robin Williams told me, If you're doing the right thing it should be fun, so if you're unhappy, you're either doing the wrong thing, or doing it the wrong way!" Wilmer Valderrama

"Robin Williams also said, greet each fan like it's the most important day of their life." Wilmer Valderrama

"The problem is, is happiness comes after success - it's a moving target, so the brain never gets there for very long. Raise success rates, happiness flatlines, raise happiness/ optimism/ deeper relationships, then success rates rise phenomenally." Shawn Achor

"*Always remember the bad you've done to others and the good others have done for you.*" *Jay Shetty*

"*What makes us both dangerous and spectacular is that we have choice.*" *Caroline Myss*

Why is it beneficial?

Being powerful is the athlete that practices at 5 am on a cold and freezing winter's morning, a cheetah that runs despite being tired, the manager that stands up for the underdog with the risk of losing their job. For reasons like this then, having extraordinary commitment or resilience or just pure belief in others allows you to thrive within any circumstance. You can sense a powerful person as soon as they walk into a room. They exude a presence, not necessarily a confidence or ego, but they stand firm, in their space, hold their head high and are not afraid to contribute to others or indeed stand alone without the acknowledgement of other people. This type of power comes from knowing that we live as part of a human ecosystem, a community of people and must contribute before we will receive back. A powerful person practices communication and an understanding of theirs and others' emotions which allows them to engender trusting relationships and leads to success. People will always want to work and spend time with you as they know you will be genuinely interested in them being heard, including what is important for them and their well-being.

"*Because what you don't own, owns you. Being real is the first step to being great.*" Lolly Daskal, The Leadership Gap

"*Not finance. Not strategy. Not technology. It is teamwork that remains the ultimate competitive advantage, both because it is so powerful and so rare.*" Patrick Lencioni

My journey with Power:

BEFORE I DISCOVERED POWER: At his Transformational Show 'When the world is falling apart do this' in 2016, Kyle Cease said we live in a world which tells Hollywood stories. We invent a reason to not feel good and push ourselves down; then the adventure becomes about overcoming and then succeeding at what had us beat so we can feel better about ourselves. So what we actually conquer is us finding ourselves back at the original place that we were at. Do we no longer have the capacity to live in the uncomfortable - set continuous goals and expectations that stretch us, play with failure, and not care what others think about how we look? A false sense of security and political correctness has us play small and ultimately avoid experiences that would lead to transformational performance. You only need to watch survival programmes on television to see how people become alive again when their current daily situation and habits are challenged by adapting to a new situation or skill set.

POWER was my discovering what were the emotional stories I lived in and since doing my first coaching course in 2013, I was able to start becoming more aware of how I saw myself and the world. I wanted to create my own toolset that could help me personally develop beyond where I am and some way of being able to remember what I had already learnt. A being able to bookmark how I got there so I could do it again and then share that with my coaching clients. Could the PASSION Toolset become the ability to hi-jack our thinking and the stories that keep us from venturing into the unknown? I would very much like POWER and the other tools to be the short-cut or cheat sheet for you to use in your daily life.

A lot of my not being able to access my power had come from my lack of understanding and controlling my emotions. There are a couple of well-known profiling tools like the Myers Briggs Type Indicator with it's concept by Carl Jung and developed by Katharine Cook Briggs and Isabel Briggs Myers; and the DISC behaviour assessment tool based on theory by Walter Clark and developed by William Moulton Marston. In both tools I score highly in the areas of Dominance and Extroversion plus a high score in Intuition and Influencing. Now these all being great qualities, the areas missing are Steadiness, Conscientiousness and Judgments. I make a really great Debater and am very good at coming up with ideas and providing connections for people as I am the firestarter in the room for social settings and business meetings.

However, when it comes down to following through and running your family life and small business, these very strong characteristics did not stand me in good stead. What I was able to see was that my lack of self-control with my emotions was actually a loss of power - an inability to control what I said and felt in many situations, which meant I was not serving my longer-term purpose of wanting a stable family and business. Also people around me would see someone who was great at ideas and inspiring a room full of people but not so good at sticking to one idea and completing the more mundane tasks that secured on-going work.

"Your mind/ body heals at the speed of your self-esteem." Caroline Myss

"The only way to get a positive outlook is through haaardd work!" Michael R Mantell

"It's when you can love yourself, when you hate yourself; when you're still dating the wrong guy or taking rubbish from your boss, and you practice acceptance. That... is the power... that everybody wants, it's right there." Danielle La Porte.

DECISION MAKING: How we make decisions is an important element to living a powerful life. Some people are naturally good at making decisions and there is possibly a direct correlation with good decision makers and the level of success in their life. The route of poor decision making comes from environment, fear of failure and overwhelm. I have always struggled to make a decision, from the simplest of things like menu choices to deciding a time for a meeting, through to which task I should be focusing on. Decision paralysis and perfectionism are of the same side of the coin, a fear of failing. It has always been so important to me to 'get it right' that what I failed to see was there is no 'right' way to do anything, just finding the best way for you. As I read more about business entrepreneurs and having taken more actions myself, it is clear that failure is a part of that process as it provides guidance to the next crucial step to take. Without trialling something we will never know if it will work. But ultimately, a goal is never truly achieved exactly as we set out as there will always be some changes along the way. What setting a goal allows us to do is create more clarity, focus and drive so we are able to get closer to what we wish to achieve or even find out what we don't want, which we would have never discovered if we'd not tried.

Using POWER I have been able to identify when I'm delaying decisions and "just do it" as Nike say. Plus attach less emotion to the process and move forward with each stage without getting too caught up in meanings and expectations.

"*Be careful of your beliefs because they become your thoughts, and those become your feelings, which becomes your actions, become your habits, become your character and that becomes your destiny.*" *John Mattone, Steve Jobs Coach*

"*There are some leaders who just haven't discovered how to win yet. Greatness is not for the genetically chosen few, it's within all of our grasps.*" *Arnold Schwarzenegger*

"*We have the kind of power that cannot be given to us, therefore cannot be taken away. Shaping our world to reflect value and purpose.*" *Henry Kimsey-House*

DEALING WITH CHALLENGE: This was probably the area that I felt I was stronger in. I have always been the one who speaks out, doesn't agree with something to keep the peace and pretty courageous mixed with an innocence (always easier to have more courage when you think the best of everything). However, the more personal development and coaching I have invested in I have been able to see that my dealing with challenges had no strong foundations at all really. I was unsure what I really wanted and when receiving negative feedback would not know if I was right to continue representing my views. I'm sure others have different experiences and have always found it easy to deal with challenges or when facing negativity deal with it with an assuredness of what's right for them. However, the deep rootedness of this for me went back to growing up with a very strong and powerful father-figure and an assumption that my views were never the right views.

This continued surprisingly into my adult years with an unchallenged thinking that I do not have the option to disagree with the world and the only time I would, would be in a character of playfulness I invented to be able to express my disagreement. It actually led me to rejecting most commonly held views and wanting to be a loner, black sheep; which ultimately meant I dropped any structures that might have been useful. For example I saw certainty and conformity as the enemy, when actually my biggest wins using POWER to support my coaching business have been my ability to successfully integrate short and medium-term planning and dealing with the little details that are so crucial to the success of you as a business person and role model. Now I find if there is a question that needs to be asked I will ask immediately, no stone left unturned; because this allows us to actually take better care of ourselves, whereas before I would have seen it as compliance and red tape. I used to hate any form-filling, questioning, constructive criticism, rejections, challenges to my opinion; it would almost be painful for me and I would have no real constructive way of dealing with the negative emotion. Now with POWER I begin to feel a lot more comfortable around these challenges and negativity and it doesn't 'hurt' so much to deal with it anymore, it is part of making me stronger with so much improvement made in this area.

"*Stop walking through the world looking for confirmation that you don't belong. You will always find it because you've made that your mission. Stop scouring people's faces for evidence that you're not enough. You will always find it because you've made that your goal. True belonging and self-worth are not goods; we don't negotiate their value with the world. The truth about who we are lives in our hearts. Our call to courage is to protect our wild heart against constant evaluation, especially our own. No one belongs here more than you.*" Brene Brown

RELATIONSHIP TO THE EXTERNAL WORLD: Another critical element to grasping how POWER works in the real world is comparing it to the likes of a huge energy battery. Everything we do is an exchange of this energy. We go to work and are given money for our investment of energy. Mothers raise children/ future worker generations and either partners, families or the government support this investment of energy. It is not often, however, that we really look at how we will regenerate our energy apart from focusing on our sleep, exercise and good nutritional food. As a single mum bringing up two amazing children, POWER helped me to see very much that the oxygen mask needed to be put firmly and unapologetically on my face first if I was to continue to provide a high level of care and energy for the children.

Once we understand our 'self-care /fulfillment formula' we can work towards having an abundance of energy - knowing how to top it up. Rather like the entrepreneurs who talk about only needing a few hours sleep, or the stories that Muhammad Ali and Arnold Schwarzennegger tell about pushing through pain barriers to new levels of endurance. Either way it's understanding what works for each of us and then being able to push ourselves or have others push us to our next level of improvement. However, this is when we are only isolated to a risk of our own 'battery drains' which might be distractions, stress, too much analysis and generally focusing on the wrong things. It is all too easy to design a way to fill up our battery life when we are not impacted by others or the world around us.

When you add in bosses, spouses, parents, friends and general financial and circumstantial restrictions it begins to add a hefty drain to your battery energy level. This is where you take back the POWER, speak to your boss candidly, offer some compromises with spouses, talk honestly with parents and friends and have clarity and focus around your finance and other circumstances impacting you. Do a financial audit, keep a daily note of spending, know what you can and cannot buy, and when circumstances become too over-whelming, share with people you trust and ask for support. No man is an island and we need to understand what is, who is or where is our battery being drained and nip it in the bud.

> *"The reason why most people face the future with apprehension instead of anticipation is because they don't have it well designed."* Jim Rohn

QUALITIES POWER DEVELOPS and SUGGESTED ROLE MODELS: When we can learn to be powerful in our lives and relationships we can pretty much achieve anything. Powerful people are people who understand themselves and how the world around them works. However, they also have a strong sense of respecting the rules and challenging the rules as well, total contradiction. If all the inventors gave up after being told their product wouldn't work we wouldn't have the lightbulb and we certainly wouldn't think the world was round. Powerful people don't waste their time reacting to things they can't control, and bide their time with the things they can control. They measure their performance, know their weaknesses, focus on strengths and know where they want to go. Their main qualities are discipline, hardiness and finding their personal formula that works for them.

Below are examples of people I truly respect for their demonstration of POWER:

Oprah Winfrey
Tony Robbins
Arnold Schwarzenegger
Muhammad Ali
Will Smith
Ken Blanchard
Peter Drucker
Renee Mauborgne

"It's not the imbalances of life that get you down, it's doing meaningless things that aren't taking you where you want to go." Danielle la Porte

"To be trusted is a greater compliment than being loved." George Macdonald.

"I hated every minute of training, but I said, don't quit. Suffer now and live the rest of your life as a champion." Muhammad Ali

"What drives learning is curiosity and collaboration." Sir Ken Robinson

"*Contract for your own leadership style with your boss. Your boss is not a mind reader, take responsibility and communicate.*" Marshall Goldsmith

"*If we start the day as a leader. Why do we expect things to go smoothly for us as follower? What if our planner selects the situational need.*" Marshall Goldsmith

"*Long-range planning does not deal with the future decisions, but with the future of present decisions.*" Peter Drucker

"*Time management systems become obsessive, driven by the need to be more acceptable/ productive. The guiding question is does this sustain me?*" Danielle la Porte

How you'd know when it's present?

- ☐ You are not rushed to make a decision when pressurised
- ☐ You know that when something negative happens that it is not final and that there will always be another option
- ☐ You listen and pay attention to the present moment as you know this is where you will find answers and opportunities
- ☐ You are considerate about external things but do not base your identity or self-esteem on external things
- ☐ You do not NEED anything but appreciate EVERYTHING
- ☐ You are extremely humble and observant and use these qualities to impact situations positively if you can
- ☐ You are not afraid to put yourself first (this is not selfishness, there is a certain amount of taking care of yourself before you can take care of others) and are happy to make a hard decision that might upset others because you have their best intention at heart

Follow me!

"Marshall Goldsmith said "Peter Drucker taught me not to prove how smart or right we are, but the most important lesson is to make a difference.""

"There's nothing like a sense of entitlement to repel what you want the most." Daniele la Porte

"Rule to success - there are no rules. All that is created is created by people no smarter than you or me. When you understand that, you remove limitations and fail forward." Mark Fitt

"Magic moves we can use- apologise/ ask for help/ show optimism/ ask active Qs - they trigger decent behaviour in people." Marshall Goldsmith

How you'd know when it's not present?:

☐ You are always rushing to answer questions, please people and jump in feet first without assessing a situation

☐ When negative things happen you take them hard and personally and feel down-hearted as if it's an irreparable situation

☐ You are constantly distracted in the present moment thinking about the past or the future

☐ Other people's opinions are more important than your own - causing you to change your mind and you talk more about others' lives

☐ You NEED everything and appreciate NOTHING

☐ You don't complete things and constantly want material things to make you feel better

☐ You feel guilty about putting yourself first (this is a false economy) and you hate making hard decisions that upset others. But ultimately the 'not making a decision' is still a decision in itself and possibly causes more harm

"*Feeling is understanding. If you feel good, you take on what people are asking you to do. Focus on making people feel good.*" Wim Hof, The Iceman

"Yesterday I was clever, so I wanted to change the world. Today I am wise, so I am changing myself." Rumi

"Learn to say no to the good, so you can say yes to the best." John C Maxwell

"Sports/ Business does not build character. It reveals it." Heywood Broun

"Everything that irritates us about others can lead us to an understanding about ourselves." Carl Jung

"Do you want a Mentor? Mentorship isn't just a face to face or 1-2-1 dimension. You don't have to meet them to be mentored by them." Marie Forleo

"The trick about advice, the minute I start to say it like its wisdom, it's then like - what works for me, works for you, no!" Mike Rowe @mikeroweworks

"*Don't follow your passion, take it with you wherever you go. But don't be so damn picky about what you apply it to!*" Mike Rowe, TV Broadcaster

"*The man was explaining that his wife had Alzheimers disease, and for the past 5 years she hasn't known who he is. The doctor was surprised and asked the man why he continues to go faithfully if she has no idea who he is....the old man replied, because I still know who she is.*" Quote from Facebook @NeverForget

Legendary Rob Dyrdek points out, "*learning how to fill up your cup with good energy, every day, is the real key to success. And he adds - but gratitude does you no good when you're half empty.*" Interviewed by Lewis Howes

Daily Calibration Tool:

Just like the little guy on the front cover - it is crucial to be at the source of our own power, the place where you recharge and are able to fill yourself up. For some this is exercise, for some it is the arts and for others it's just remembering to structure every day to achieve the things that will make you feel fulfilled. (Remember you don't have to be having fun to feel fulfilment). Here are some questions to ask yourself daily to check YOUR BATTERY LEVELS. You've been told, this is the most vital part of the PASSION toolset. Without energy we cannot look after ourselves or then give back to others.

1. Am I confident during my day/ with this meeting/ with this situation/ with this conversation?

2. What is my intention here in this moment?

3. Am I remembering to be present/ have an anchor to remind myself to be present?

4. Name something I like about myself?

5. Am I being proactive or playful versus reactive?

"Who looks outside, dreams; who looks inside, awakes." Carl Jung

"Nobody's going to give you permission to invent the future." Jame Altucher

"There's no such thing as a bad business climate just inappropriate leadership." Lynne Copp, Worklife (Taken from Billy Connolly)

"*People who wonder if the glass is half empty or half full miss the point. The glass is refillable.*" Unknown

"*What emotion do I want to infect today? And be honest when I feel off, as that's when you can catch theirs.*" Vanessa van Edwards

"*Authentic leaders demonstrate a passion for their purpose, practice their values consistently, and lead with their hearts as well as their heads.*" George, Sims, McLean and Mayer 2007

"*Attitude is everything, so pick a good one.*" Wayne Dyer

"*Everyone you meet is fighting a battle you know nothing about. Be kind. Always.*" The Ancient One from Doctor Strange

"Don't fight the flow of the river, surrender to it and then use its power." The Ancient One from Doctor Strange

"Higher functioning people don't put their attention on what is." Wayne Dyer

"Life is like riding a bicycle. To keep your balance you must keep moving." Albert Einstein

"When your fear touches someone's pain it becomes pity and when your love touches someone's pain it becomes compassion." Steven Levine.

"Thought goes into form at the speed of your history." Caroline Myss

"I am the world's top rank executive coach I am too cowardly and undisciplined to do this on my own. You quit because you get bored and it's hard to face the reality of your life every day. Get over that shame thing, it's okay to need help. It just takes courage and 2 minutes a day." Marshall Goldsmith

"Rather than searching for life's meaning always know that you have the power to create it." Marie Forleo

"Dirty jobs reconnected me to what's fundamentally important. We are not connected to that 3 million people feed 300 million people 3 times a day! We touch a button and light comes on, in every place! We get toilets, hot water, cold air. We are no longer gobsmacked by all of this." Mike Rowe

"Behaviour alone is not enough, the energy, the soul that you infuse into your actions, it matters. This moment creates your future moment." Marie Forleo

"Are you the person who is living in the state you talk about, you're making that reality true to you. And then make that reality true for another." Krishnaji, One World Academy

"We live on a blue planet that circles around a ball of fire next to a moon that moves the sea, and you don't believe in miracles." Unknown

"If you hate, then you've been defeated." Confucius

"What's it going to take you to say the kindest thing. The answer is incredible, it'll take all of us, being all of who we are." Danielle laPorte

What changes will you make after reading this chapter?:

pAssion

Chapter 2

AUTHENTICITY -

Knowing what your specific magic powers are

AUTHENTICITY - knowing what your specific magic powers are

DEFINITION:

This is all about your 'happy place', where, what or whoever that involves. An authentic person understands his/her values. Re-creates them regularly and always uses these principles to guide what they do in/ outside a business. Always has clarity before committing to things. If your values are not met then action is needed, not resentment. Change the value or change the environment.

"*Your goal is to rebuild the connection with yourself and turn the volume up on your own intuition.*" Catherine Collaut

"*Is happiness what we all seek because the definition might be seen as short-term pleasure. Long-term happiness comes from joy and meaningful actions and where you won't always feel happy when you're being purposeful.*" Shawn Achor

"*The opposite of happiness isn't unhappiness, it's apathy. Ultimately unhappiness can lead to a lot of good things, a break up of an unhappy relationship etc.*" Shawn Achor

Why is it beneficial?

Being authentic is about being the real you. The problem is we have got so lost in our expectations of what is a 'good version' of ourselves and our beliefs about others' expectations of us (which usually aren't even real, as we've overreacted and assumed from things they've said), and the expectations and 'standards' we see from the world around us and social media. The more I've thought about the world in these last few years, the more damage I can see that the marketing engines of a consumer society do to our self-image and self-esteem. As we are part of a community we want to fit in and be accepted and so strive to look and sound and feel like everyone else. There is absolutely nothing wrong with wanting to have these 'connections' that is what makes us human and is perhaps the biggest gift of life - feeling a part of something. However, the problem comes when we confuse conformity with acceptance - these two couldn't be any more polar opposites. So being able to stretch the authenticity muscle and face the potential rejection along the way, has many long-term benefits. Being able to stay true to yourself, being strong in the face of rejection (which is huge, think of the increase in suicide rates with social media bullying) and so much happier moving away from people who are not like you and towards the ones you finally find yourself with who challenge and support you.

"Do not be dismayed by the brokenness of the world. All things break. And all things can be mended. Not with time, as they say, but with intention. So go. Love intentionally, extravagantly, unconditionally. The broken world waits in darkness for the light that is you." LR Knost

"If you bring forth what is within you, what you bring forth will save you. If you do not bring forth what is within you, what you do not bring forth will destroy you." St Thomas

"South african phrase - Sawubona- I see you and when I see you I bring you into being."

"Your attitude is a self-fulfilling prophecy." Marc Benioff, Salesforce

My journey with Authenticity:

DECISION MAKING: One of my students said the other day that the PASSION toolset has allowed the re-inventing of herself. Perhaps a bold claim, but my main design premise was to make personal development and coaching simple and easy to use. Much of this comes from getting students to focus on a simple daily action and making it, not about results as this causes an emotional and confrontational response and usually means we end up getting de-motivated. When we look at making decisions it all starts with how we currently feel about ourselves and view ourselves in relation to the world. Another of my students has loved the AUTHENTICITY part of the Toolset as this is where she had got unstuck in life, she had got so bogged down by the way she should be, the way things should be and as she said in our first coaching call was completely lost. She had forgotten who she was and using AUTHENTICITY has allowed her to give herself permission to be herself again.

For me AUTHENTICITY had been about a six year discovery of who I wanted to be as a mother, coach and how I want to contribute and receive back from the world. The latter has been the hardest part. I have never asked for any emotional support from potential partners because since my childhood I had limited ability to express my views if they differed from the strong views of my father. So totally unconsciously I developed a zero expectation of emotional contribution back from the world as previously it was never an even exchange, i.e. you have this opinion, this is my opinion and they are both valid. My adult relationships were about significance and duty as opposed to love and connection. This has meant a shutting myself off and only choosing what the world saw about me, I wanted to show I was strong and can do it all alone. The first casualty was my marriage to my children's father. It was inevitable, I didn't know how to be vulnerable with him and as soon as 'duty' was called into question he was out, didn't stand a chance. I acknowledge that I'm sorry he got caught up in this storm and have apologised to him years ago.

However, I think where I began to see the biggest negative impact was the relationship with my son. He has always struggled in school and he was finding senior school very hard. I was using control and command as a parenting skill and this was not working, because if you tell him to go one way, he will go completely the opposite way, just purely as a reaction to a heavy-handed approach. This challenged everything I knew about my construct of relationships which I believed was: men did things for you because of what you have provided or what they owe in the context of a dutiful relationship. My son pushed all of this out - for the first time ever I had to be vulnerable, face the mouth of the lion and stick my head in. I did this because he is my son and there is unconditional love. In the face of his rejecting my asking him to do homework, answering teachers requests, and generally pulling his weight, I had to find a new method, I had to love him unconditionally and not be afraid that he would not return my love or indeed requests. What happened was he began to see I really cared, I would ask why he was struggling rather than tell him my opinion and then feeling supported he would start to do the work. This was because I allowed him the freedom to be himself which was not what I had received. I broke down in front of him once saying I was so sad that I had shouted at him and once made him scared of me and that I didn't want to be the parent who doesn't allow him to have his own opinion. This was the making of my AUTHENTICITY and I was able to stare my biggest enemy, vulnerability, in the face and say do with me what you wish and I will still be here because I love you.

Exploring this with conditional love is my next step and one I am being honest about with a guy I am dating. This, like one of the tools for you, will be work in progress.

"*People who don't take risks generally make about two big mistakes a year. People who do take risks generally make about two big mistakes a year.*" Peter Drucker

"*Discomfort is the price of admission to a meaningful life.*" Susan David

"*Everything you do or don't do leaves a print on your self-esteem.*" John Assaraf

DEALING WITH CHALLENGE: As a big part of my growing up was related to impressing a strong role model, then I'm sure you can imagine that most of my life became about other's expectations and impressing them. Although that wasn't my father's intention as we have had this conversation and he has said he just wanted me to be happy. It never is that way though is it- we think we give off a certain feeling, but that's not how it's interpreted by others. So when dealing with challenge historically, I would back down thinking that my opinion was automatically wrong and it felt uncomfortable being with negative feelings so I would automatically try to say something nice. But actually it's about being able to allow yourself to 'breathe' into the negative space and be with it as a type of learning for you and the other person. I am always too quick to want to make the other person feel comfortable, an incessant pleasing nature. What I have seen from just being with a lack of instant approval from others in their responses: they might not smile back, they might say something negative to you - that it's 100% not about you and is something that's going on in their head.

This is the same in public places when people have come across a negative reaction from someone; it will always be that the other person is having a bad day and you were on the receiving end. Obviously, it's worth saying something if it's of value to you and the people around you, but most of the time worth considering, how much energy are you going to lose by challenging something that another is not even aware of?

"*Even if things are going great or you have this big win, doesn't mean that the day to day is still easy.*" *Suzy Batiz*

"*We make our goals try to fit with what society says. We should be taking our goals and make everything fit that.*" *Hunter Thompson*

"*We're in this moment of high leverage with social media, but just watch cat videos or wine about our boss. We can connect with a billion people worldwide but we chose not to.*" *Seth Goddin*

"*The planet does not need more successful people. The planet desperately needs more peacemakers, healers, restorers, storytellers and lovers of all kinds.*" *Dalai Lama*

"*A merry heart doeth good like a medicine, but a broken spirit dryeth the bones.*" *King Soloman*

RELATIONSHIP TO THE EXTERNAL WORLD: Another part of my learning to be completely AUTHENTIC has been showing myself to the world and what I love and not needing any type of approval, just share because this is who I am. I see in posts on social media this kind of authenticity - it can be rare as we all fall into the trap of, will people like me, at some stage now and again. This is because, despite all of our failings as humans we are inextricably connected to each other, we do not exist alone, we exist through relationships and contributing. "The connection cannot be broken BUT our belief in the connection is constantly tested and repeatedly severed." Brene Brown. We need to feel connected to the world to be able to stand alone, it gives us the courage to be ourselves, to believe in ourselves and in others.

Einstein said: "*The intuitive mind is a sacred gift, and the rational mind a faithful servant. We have created a society that honours the servant and has forgotten the gift.*"

"*The real problem is usually two or three questions deep. If you want to go after someone's problem, be aware that most people aren't going to reveal what the real problem is after the first question.*" Jim Rohn

"*Give 100% focus and energy = become an irresistible force, not an immovable object. Where have you decided you can be an amateur vs a professional?*" Marshall Goldsmith

"*Greatness is a by-product of vulnerability but most people are afraid to be vulnerable.*" Jay Abraham

QUALITIES AUTHENTICITY DEVELOPS and SUGGESTED ROLE MODELS: Authentic people are real, they are not afraid to show themselves, be themselves and accept and celebrate others for who they also are and what they have also achieved. They accept the world for what it is, not for how they think it should be. However, that doesn't mean they are content with staying the same and not wanting to change, improve or even challenge when their values are questioned. It is a fine balance between acceptance, letting go and dealing with a certain amount of pushing back and friction. Generally, authentic people are on purpose because they know themselves well, what their strengths are and are not scared to go get what they want. They are also not afraid of hard work or falling down because they know this is part of achieving what is ultimately an expression of who you are (the concept of success coming easier to you when you're doing what you love, positive energy attracting positive energy).

Below are examples of people I truly respect for their demonstration of AUTHENTICITY:
Marie Forleo
Glennon Doyle Melton
Elizabeth Gilbert
Cheryl Strayed
Maya Angelou

"Are you leveraging your full potential? If not either your beliefs about what you do have to change or do we know ourselves that well?" Jonathan Fields

"We think we have to work hard for love. Our capacity for love is vast. We hold back as fear limits us to a smaller version of us." Henry Kimsey-House

"People are wise in proportion not to their experience, but in their capacity to experience." George Bernard Shaw

"Serving is not transactional it's relational. To find what's needed - look for where people are right; it's not about hanging each other out to dry." Henry Kimsey-House

"*In relationships we look for differences, then start to separate ourselves. INSTEAD.. Look why we're doing it all. Say, "yes and...", so it's not disguised as a but!* Karen Kimsey-House

"*Rewards by their very nature narrow our focus.*" Daniel H Pink

"*Economic survival and personal fulfilment used to depend on withholding your natural expression. Now it depends solely on this.*" Daniel H Pink

"*A sense of being on the same side. Totally present with the person that is actually here, not the person we WISH we're here.*" Henry Kimsey-House

How you'd know when it's present?

☐ You make decisions only based on serving your values, which are the beliefs you hold about yourself and the world

☐ When something negative happens you do not question yourself and look to see what you can impact moving forward

☐ You appreciate differences of opinions, constructive criticism and are not quick to react, you pause and deal with what happens

☐ You embrace differences in the world, are excited to learn how people differ from you and celebrate friction (challenge is where we excel and perform as people)

☐ You can be okay with your negatives and comfortable to talk about your achievements

☐ You are proud of who you are and express this within your community; using it to positively impact yours and others' environments

☐ You are not afraid to stand up for your beliefs even if this means losing friends, support and not being part of that community

"Socially responsible businesses are now not about seeking profit, they are more about ethics as a code. They actually have purpose as the catalyst rather than the objective."
Daniel H Pink

"Managers came back with green indicators on every task - Alan Mullaly CEO at the time for Ford's reply was, "What task are you winning, losing $17billion?!" Marshall Goldsmith

Margaret Fuller - "Explore the whole of you and there you will find your art form."

"The Secret - Do what you say you're going to do. Aim for impeccable. Words are arrows. When you can't honour your word say so." Danielle la Porte

How you'd know when it's not present?

- ☐ You make decisions based on other people's values and beliefs of the world and are not aware of what you hold true
- ☐ When something negative happens you react, look to blame and resent people and the world (victim)
- ☐ Differences of opinions, criticism and comments make you constantly defend yourself and hide
- ☐ You try to conform or control others and shun people for their differences. Change and friction is a threat
- ☐ You are reliant on receiving praise and acceptance and still never appreciate anything about yourself or others
- ☐ Given the opportunity you change your views and opinions based on what you hear from the outside world
- ☐ You constantly remind people of what you have sacrificed for them, and make it seem like you had no choice (martyr)

"It's hard to practice compassion when our own worthiness and authenticity is off balance." Brene Brown.

"You are the expert on you. If you/ your company are not having some polarising effect you're not showing up." Danielle la Porte

Daily Calibration Tool:

Now as important as power is, AUTHENTICITY is an add-on if you like. This is the place where we find OUR LINE IN THE SAND and then we are able to communicate this eloquently to others we work, live and socialise with. Once we have this skill it is easy to understand: what makes us and others tick, when others cross our line and when we cross others' lines we will immediately be able to understand what is and is not working for us and them. If AUTHENTICITY is done well it allows amazing communication and team building, done badly will cause resentment, blame and gossiping.

	What's most important to me & why	How would I rate this compared to the others
eg	Accuracy, I like detail and I like to know I have taken my time on a piece of work and considered all areas and seen it through to completion.	VI
	Consideration & respect from others. I am a very respectful person and take my time to listen to other people and provide them what they need, so expect the same in return	IV
	Quiet environments. I can concentrate well in these type of scenarios and do my best work. I enjoy my own company	VII
	Visibility of processes and structure. I thrive with people who work this way and like to have a home environment with rules and rewards, this helps motivate me	V
	I enjoy time on my hobbies as it allows me to focus and become better at my skills that I get a lot of enjoyment from, including coding, fishing and quantum mechanics	VIII
	Feedback from others. I enjoy this as it allows me to improve and also please others	I
	Communication, because I feel more comfortable knowing what others think	III
	Safety, because I can relax when I know I'm in an environment I can trust and feel protected by the people in it	II

Please see the blue box as an example of how you can find your values (you don't have to have eight values). Then the purple box opposite is YOUR TURN. Write in pencil and then you can re-try this again in the future. Using a tally system - mark an 'I' for each time you rate one value as higher than another value. Go all the way down your list comparing the first value with the second then the first with the third etc. Then do the second value with the third, second with the fourth etc until you've compared all values. Then add up the highest ranked value on a scale from I to VIII. (VIII is the highest.) Ask yourself if you are achieving your top three values?

	What value is most important to me & why?	How would I rate this value compared to my other values? (rate on a scale from I to VIII most important?)
1		
2		
3		
4		
5		
6		
7		
8		

"*We look for the When and the How - it's the What and the Why which are important. It doesn't work when we try to control outcome and timing.*" E Fletcher

"*Why do people try to feel grateful? So they can feel nice about it? But at the same time, blame everyone for their suffering; total paradox.*" Krishnaji, One World Academy

"*IBM, a huge computer power operates with just three core right brain thinking parts: Dignity, Service and Excellence. That way when everything else changes these still remain the same as they are agreed.*" Stephen Covey, 7 habits of highly effective people.

"*We're lending money we don't have, to kids who are training for jobs, that don't exist. Believing hard work is the enemy, not smart work.*" Mike Rowe

"*We shall not cease from exploration and at the end of all our exploring, will be to arrive where we started and know the place for the first time.*" TS Eliot

"*When you care about how you feel you can become it here and now.*" Abraham Hicks

"You were born with an inner guidance system that tells you when you are on or off purpose by the amount of joy you are experiencing. The things that bring you the greatest joy are in alignment with your purpose." Jack Canfield

"We associate gentleness and tenderness with ourselves as a kind of slack or letting ourselves off the hook. Only when I'm gentle can I let go and do the work." Cheryl Strayed

"Don't be impressed by money, degrees, titles and followers. Be Impressed by integrity, creativity, selflessness and courage." Unknown

"Profit is always a result, more importantly what's your cause, your belief, that's what drives customers in." Simon Sinek

"Do sharks complain about Mondays? No. They're up early, biting and chasing s***, being scary and reminding everyone that they're a flipping shark." Anonymous

"Want to know what your biggest problem is, you think you shouldn't have any." Tony Robbins

"Go where the resonance is." Danielle la Porte

"Broken things hold us down. Go have the conversation you've been avoiding." Vanessa Van Edwards

What changes will you make after reading this chapter?:

paSsion

Chapter 3

SAYING WHAT YOU WILL DO

Not being afraid to try

SAYING WHAT YOU WILL DO - not being afraid to try

Definition:

Fear and Overwhelm have us play small/ find it hard to commit. You don't complete things, are late on projects, or are ignorant to your impact of what you've said. This diminishes you bit by bit. Masters thrive on learning from failure and recommit to/ let go of goals and principles that do/ don't serve them.

"Perfectionism is a serial killer. It is fear in high heeled shoes." Elizabeth Gilbert

Why is it beneficial?

Someone who is always saying what they will do shouldn't be confused with an 'Action Junkie', i.e. what I mean by this is, you will hear people all the time say, "yes I'm so busy, I'm rushed off my feet". Being busy is the opposite extreme of the scale to someone who will consistently say what they are going to do. Because if you are effective in saying what you will do you should never find yourself too busy, as you will only be agreeing to things that stretch you as oppose to completely stress you out. So in actual fact, when you effectively say what you will do, you agree to do things that you know you will complete and you understand that you may feel overwhelmed at times and even face failure but accept this as part of the course when saying what you are going to do. You also understand that your words are powerful and will impact others' worlds, so are never quick to 'give your word' to any actions without first considering how this will impact you and others around you. Plus you know how important it is to communicate any delays, deviations and changes from the original plan. Once you master this, you become a trusted friend, colleague and even advisor to some. People will love your clarity of vision, action and communication and begin to mirror what you do.

"Success is normally found in a pile of mistakes." Tim Fargo, @alphabetsuccess

"Only when stress is values aligned, is when we contribute." Susan David

My journey with Saying what you will do:

DECISION MAKING: This was an interesting one for me because I had never held myself to account in my 20s, it was about experiencing life and emotions and anything related to measures and capturing information was tedious, boring and suffocating. A lack of responsibility is okay for a five year old but I was entering my 30s with children and a husband. I also had never had someone brave enough to hold me to account before - remember the reference to putting my head inside the lion's mouth - we always use characteristics to describe how we see the external world when it is actually us we are describing. ROAR! So after completing a leadership course over four years ago, I began to book things in my phone calendar, created a huge flipchart in the family kitchen so we could jointly plan things and begin to write down: what actions I was setting for the day, what I achieved each day and sending daily morning texts to an accountability buddy.

Although this seems pretty mundane and doesn't set the world on fire, what it was teaching me to do was document who I was, what I wanted to achieve and most importantly what I could be counted on for. That means I am beholdant to others, they have expectations of me and what I have promised to do. No longer was the story in my mind: why should I do anything for others, the world tells me what to do and how to live my life so why should I do anything for a world that doesn't accept me for who I am. Obviously, we have established this is the made up story of a five year old and in letting this go and sharing with others what I can contribute and what I would like them to contribute in response, I can begin to have an adult relationship with the world.

Now possibly this may appear another basic concept but we assume becoming an adult is something that most people do naturally. Many people disguise themselves as grown-ups with grown-up problems and lives, but most of their issues with the world are hidden behind a lack of clarification about what it is they are supposed to be contributing and what it is in THEIR head that they have communicated to the world that they expect in return. This causes stress, resentment and most of the complaining, disgruntled behaviour in the world.

So where SAYING WHAT YOU WILL DO starts is with clearly stating who you are, what you want and how that will work for others. This doesn't always lead to immediate agreement and resolution of any problem, but at least we can begin to see where the real potential challenges are. Then deal with them a lot more effectively than a 'fake problem' because people don't want to offend other people by upsetting them or being confrontational. It is about leading the way and being prepared to put your head above all the other poppies, the tall poppy syndrome. The leaders will set the example and know for sure others will always be quick to question when they haven't done what they said they'd do, but the questioners will never be the first to say what they will do. Be prepared to be shot down and not appreciated as this is the price of saying what you will do. Although it may seem like the majority of people are negatively judging, actually people are impressed with this type of behaviour and would rather follow someone who is courageous to say what they will do, than someone who is not honest about what they have not been able to do, sets no goals and plays small.

"*Success is not final, failure is not fatal, it's the courage to continue that counts.*" Winston Churchill

"*We are born and we die, so we have a right to choose what happens in the middle. Also rejection is the pathway to success.*" Shep Gordon, US celebrity agent

DEALING WITH CHALLENGE: This is an attribute I have been able to begin mastering over the past few years. When dealing with setbacks where I am stopped from making decisions or taking certain actions because of an intervening factor/ someone has let me down; previously these situations would have thrown me and I would be so affected as to not know what action to take. I would be very used to fighting to get my own way, that disappointment wasn't really in my vocabulary. Now learning to love curveballs means that I accept more when things don't go my way and I look at different options which actually could mean a better scenario or improved strengths for myself. After all, disruptive technologies are proving to be an insurmountable threat to traditional business models because they thrive on replacing established structures. Know the rules but be prepared to adapt when needs be, or even re-invent the rules. Just remind yourself to ride it out, be patient and it might not be as bad as you expect.

"*I can accept failure, everyone fails at something. But I can't accept not trying.*" Michael Jordan

"*Fear is a far more dominant force in human behaviour than euphoria.*" Alan Greenspan

RELATIONSHIP TO THE EXTERNAL WORLD: The key thing here is having an unbreakable vision, but that is easier said than done. I used to consistently question myself, what I am good at, what career I should and shouldn't have and where I should be going. Notice the amounts of *should!* People with unbreakable visions never have *should* in their mindset it is entirely about a passion for solving a real problem and nothing will get in their way as they have an assuredness about the difference they are making and the value they will bring. "You don't have to love what you do, just be passionate about the problem that you're solving, why you're solving it and the potential of the solution" Jon Lee, Founder Rabbut

The starting point is to properly question your values and that those values are being expressed in what you say you are doing. You can stick at other things but ultimately the road will always lead you back to where you are really headed. Once you are focused doing something you are great at, it is so much easier to maintain that vision with whatever life has to throw at you. You're unstoppable, it is not always fun, but it is so much more fulfilling than doing the wrong thing.

"You only achieve focus when you've done it." Jay Abraham

"Discovering what's important is a gift. With a problem, use the Wheel of Change and choose where to: Create/ Preserve/ Eliminate/ Accept." Marshall Goldsmith

QUALITIES THAT SAYING WHAT YOU WILL DO DEVELOPS AND SUGGESTED ROLE MODELS: These people are the straight talkers and do what they say they are going to do, no matter what. They are the ones you want on the battle field with you so to speak. They are responsible, caring and great leaders. They walk their talk, this is critical. Much of modern leadership has been based around good marketing - having a good set of company values/vision/beliefs and yet do most of the leadership teams model these behaviours, not often. Transparency then is key, once you state clearly what you will do it allows others to trust you and believe that they are safe in your hands. These types of people are also very good at measuring and testing what works and getting others to do the same. They are not infallible, make mistakes, hold their hands up and then move forward with new information learnt from experience.

Below are examples of people I truly respect for their demonstration of SAYING WHAT THEY WILL DO:

Marshall Goldsmith
Jim Collins
Simon Sinek
Peter Drucker
Ken Blanchard

"*7 Ways to Turbo Charge your Brain:*

1/Do a Single Task - We degrade brain functioning when we multi-task

2/Inhibit Information - Twice as much information available than 50 years ago = overwhelm

3/Detox Distractions - We work only for 3 mins between interruptions

4/Big Idea Thinking - Take ideas from disparate areas and synthesise

5/Calibrate Mental Effort - We spend too much time on unimportant areas

6/Innovation - Brain likes something new.. and finally..

7/ Motivation - Always trumps talent, and is fuelled by innovation."
Sandra Bond Chapman

How you'd know when it's present?

☐ You only agree to things you know you can fulfil on, always clarify expectations and never make assumptions

☐ When something negative happens you do not drop what you are doing and are honest if you need to take extra time to complete and communicate this with others

☐ You allow yourself to be open to the present moment and new opportunities but never let this distract from focusing on your commitments

☐ You base the things you say you are going to do around a bigger purpose and will always consider others

☐ Your decision for important actions is never based on just a short-term NEED and will look to satisfy a longer-term fulfilment

☐ You are more methodical in your decisions and have a strength around not giving your word to just anything

☐ You are not afraid to look bad if you do not commit to what people are asking of you. You are also not afraid to try and possibly fail as you know this is where you will learn the most

"*There is almost no such thing as ready. There is only now. And you may as well do it now. Generally speaking, now is as good a time as any.*" Hugh Laurie

"*If you've never failed, you've never tried anything new.*" George Takei

"*When I face difficulties I wonder if it was because I did something wrong, but most of the time it was because I did something right.*" Sybille Greiner

"*Nobody is consistently fearless, ever, anywhere. All we can have is consistent forward action.*" Petra Nunzi

How you'd know when it's not present?

- [ ] You agree to multiple projects, requests and favours to make others happy and never think about how this will impact your workload or life or how others will feel if you do not complete what you said you would do
- [ ] When there is a negative situation that impacts you doing what you said you were going to do, you give up and deflect it back to your environment, i.e. 'the dog ate my homework'
- [ ] You make decisions in the present moment and do not stop to think about anything beyond the short-term or yourself
- [ ] Others' opinions are more important than your own causing you to change your mind and you talk more about others' lives
- [ ] Your decision for action is always based on needs, short-term gratification and proving yourself to others
- [ ] You over-commit, are flustered and confused - you do not understand when things do not go your way or people lose trust in you
- [ ] You feel bad when you cannot complete on things you said, so you lie, use excuses, cover things up and avoid conversations

"Action is the antidote to fear." Marie Forleo

"Nobody's going to give you permission to invent the future." James Altucher

Daily Calibration Tool:

So how do you create a tool for someone that is not used to holding themselves or having someone hold them to account? There are many ways you can do this without having to pay lots of money to a coach or mentor.

1/ You can ring around local business leaders and ask if they'd mentor you for free. Many do and it's worth asking.

2/ You can ask an equally keen bean friend who is into goal setting if they'd be your ACCOUNTABILITY BUDDY.

3/ You can hold yourself to account and write a few goals at the beginning of the day but you must check these off each day. Personally I have used an accountability buddy religiously for 4 years. EVERY SINGLE DAY I text her before 9 a.m. what I am doing that day to build towards my goal achievements. It can look something like this and there are no rules except one - DO IT DAILY or else you are not practicing the muscle of SAYING WHAT YOU'RE GOING TO DO.

> **25 May 2018**
> Integrity. Kids. Dog. Entrepreneur lunch meeting. Meeting with science parks x
>
> **26 May 2018**
> Integrity. Holly to bus. Chill. Pick up holly x
>
> How did your meetings go yesterday?
>
> My meetup had 13 registered 5 of us in total. Going to try a different time maybe like morning not lunch.
> The science park she was time wasting we think
>
> Oh. The science park sounds good though. Shame it was what it was.
>
> **27 May 2018**
> Indeed. Early text. Chill see friends x
>
> **28 May 2018**
> Integrity. Dog exercise. Holly friends. Set work for week x

"Lack of clarity on a goal means lack of motivation when the s**t hits the fan." Lucy Johnson

"*The key to life isn't getting rid of struggles, it's finding worthy struggles. When we deal with problems we find happiness.*" Mark Manson

"*The reason children are happy is because they don't have a file in their mind called all the things that could go wrong.*" Marianne Williamson

What changes will you make after reading this chapter?:

PAS**S**ION

Chapter 4

STICKING TO WHAT YOU SAY

Respons-able

STICKING TO WHAT YOU SAY - respons-able

Definition:
We always wish we'd done it differently, others do it better and we never acknowledge our special skills. Masters are present, appreciate, acknowledge and focus on the long term.

"*What has you finish something is not discipline, it is self-forgiveness.*" Elizabeth Gilbert, Big Magic

"*Success is messy.. Wisdom comes from paradoxes- lucky breaks and pounding the pavement.*" Danielle la Porte

Why is it beneficial?

This skill can be aptly summed up by 'the proof is in the pudding', i.e. people don't believe what you say, they believe what you do. Sticking to what you say is then the PRACTICE of being powerful, and we know how hard that is because it is wrapped up in being able to eat the 'shit sandwich', Elizabeth Gilbert: taking the hard decisions, saying the things people don't want to hear, failing, looking stupid, taking risks, not fitting in and doubting yourself constantly. All of that sounds horrendous. So why would you want to feel any of that. Because at the end of all of that is 'the golden elixir', the fundamental nature of who you are, who you are inside is exactly who you are in the real world. Although in principle it seems straight forward, it is never that easy when played out in real life. Things happen that you hadn't planned for, circumstances and people change their minds and then your mood changes and you no longer wish to do what you said. People who are respons-able, are able to become aware of theirs and others' responses and still stick to what they said they would do. Although initially you might not seem popular, you will have complete self-respect and feel alive; people will respect you and you will be to them someone who is consistent, courageous, and real.

"The darkest hour is just before dawn." Thomas Fuller

"Emotions are data not directives." Susan David

My journey with Sticking to what I say:

DECISION MAKING: You're looking at someone who comes up with a new idea every five seconds and gets bored very easily, so this was a great tool to discover for my being able to create a sense of clarity, consistency and completion in my life. Sticking to what I said I would do was not easy for many reasons of which the main ones were:

1/ I was fortuitous enough that I had a lot of choice and support in my 20s and 30s so could try many new projects without having to see them through. 2/ I had no aversion to having a lack of a plan, loved variety and in fact thrived on risk-taking and uncertainty. This is great for a creative thinker who works for someone else, but I was trying to survive in the world as a sole trader and these traits were counterproductive to small business success. 3/ I was not aware of the impact my lack of responsibility had on others; until I saw how positively this impacted not only my children in doing well in school and their relationships but also have a hugely positive impact on what I wanted to achieve in business.

Now it's not that easy, you don't just SAY WHAT YOU WILL DO, then STICK TO WHAT YOU SAY. No. Life gets in the way. STICKING TO WHAT YOU SAY is more about learning to be forgiving because when you have to stick at something things will always get in the way: pressures of last minute changes, people not holding their end of the bargain up, things not happening when they were supposed to, yet you are supposed to stick to what you said. So when this happens and you have done everything you said, or maybe you haven't, it's not about drowning in your sorrows. This is where this goes wrong for most of us, because we make it emotional and sticky and don't want to tell people what's happened for chance of upsetting them. But in the long run not communicating is far more damaging.

Instead say we messed up, but at least we tried and now we have to re-promise by when will we now get done what we said we would do. No blame, no, it was their fault, maybe it was, but now all that is left, is to create new expectations because that's all people want to know is when will it now happen. And besides you will look a lot more powerful not pointing fingers and just getting on with what needs to be done. People don't care how you look they just want to know they can rely on you to deliver, whenever that may be (within reason).

"*Gifts are nothing without endurability.*" Dani Shapiro

"*Our Triggers express a tension between what we want (long term - hard work) and what we need (short term - pleasure). We write the definitions!!*" Marshall Goldsmith

"*Most people never run far enough on their first wind to find they've got a second.*" William James.

DEALING WITH CHALLENGE: So you've set expectations and maybe had to re-set expectations and it's going okay. But sometimes the grind of life gets us down and it all seems just a little overwhelming or what's the point. In being great at getting on with things you've lost your mojo. You are maybe that person everyone can count on to get things done, or maybe you're just the doer in life or your family depends on you to be this way, so then what happens now? Now you take care of you. What that looks like depends on you. I was always in the fast lane and everything had to be done now and to a certain extent that is still the way it is, it is the way I am. Quite often before at networking meetings I would meet people in the health industry that would suggest yoga or meditation or different ways to just be still and present with the moment rather than trying to get somewhere. Maybe fine for other people but I enjoy things fast, I'm an adrenaline junkie and I like things like Tae Boxing or Spinning classes.

It was only by having to learn myself from listening to many podcasts by billionaire business people, many of whom were also fast-paced, that making time every day to slow down and have thirty minutes to switch off from the outside world and your thoughts, was the only way that I could separate myself from at times damaging incessant thoughts. For me this looks like a half-hour walk with my dog across a meadow in the middle of the beautiful Cambridgeshire countryside. I grew up with farmland all around me and this is my 'spirit or happy place' if you like, I feel at home walking past cows and sheep and it fills me up with good feelings and is where I feel at peace. It was initially strange for me as I didn't feel I 'needed' to do this exercise as I wasn't obviously drained, however, every day I do it I feel better and realise just how much I'm always in my head, going over what I should have done or should be doing.

I wanted to explain how it works for me as it's important everyone finds their own daily version of being peaceful in a demanding world that requires you to be available to it's needs 24/7, you need to be able to say this thirty minutes is my time and nothing intervenes. Meditation or being present etc., call it what you want, but this muscle of being able to put yourself first for a few minutes is critical to your thriving. And until you see that, you won't be able to get the best out of PASSION. The whole martyrdom, I'm doing this for others is attention seeking and someone who is looking for approval and appreciation. It is important when using the PASSION toolset that you understand the toolset is here to serve as a way of you finding the source for your energy and being able to generate that for yourself. If you are constantly depending on others to provide you feelings of mental and physical support you will become very dependent on certain people. It's less of a co-dependency and more about inspiring a sense of collaboration. If people are feeling they owe you something they will resent you, whereas if you do something just because you want to and know you are at the source of your own happiness, this is a very healthy way for relationships to grow.

"*The answer to the question 'how' is 'yes'!* Laura Whitworth

"*We only have to practice being present to see how not present we are. Our minds wander like an unruly puppy that refuses to sit.*" Karen Kimsey-House

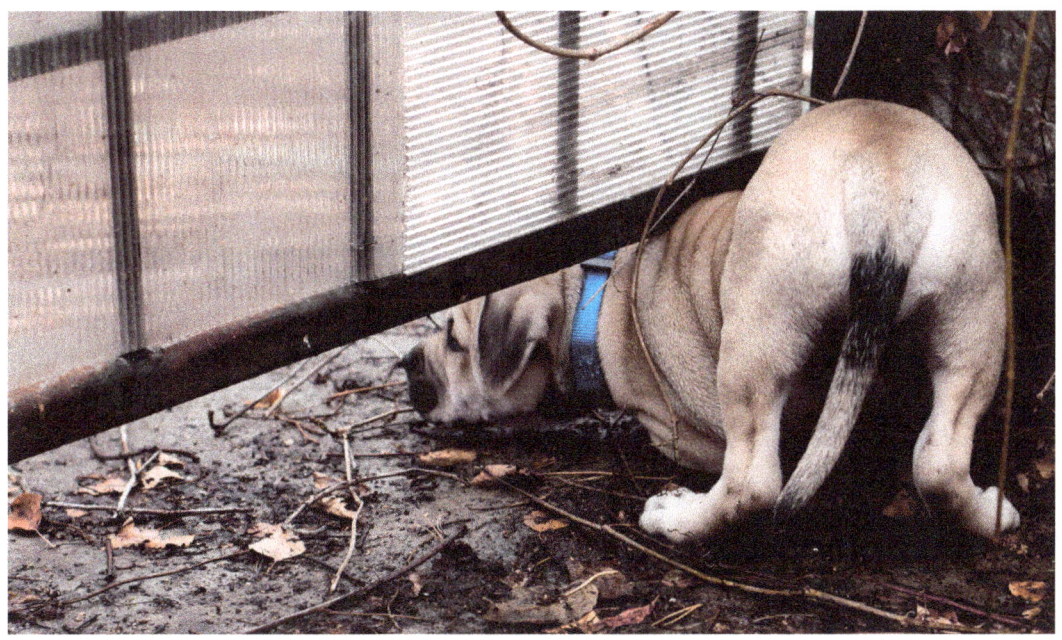

RELATIONSHIP TO THE EXTERNAL WORLD: The whole self-nurturing is great to do and easy in isolation as it is only challenging your set ways and habits. But when we relate STICKING TO WHAT WE SAY to our relationship with the rest of the world this is where the sticky hits the fan. In taking care of ourselves, there will be times where we need to hold people to account on things they may have promised. Simple enough? Not really. We don't like having to say, 'errmm you promised me that document would be done and now it will impact my work', because saying this will make us look too demanding and make the other person feel awkward around us. With parenting I have to remind myself to remind my children when they have promised to do things. It's hard enough remembering to do my tasks and then setting tasks for the kids is okay, but then it's, did they finish that homework they said they'd do, did they stick to the revision plan that we created together? This is hard work. Why have I got to hold them to account? Because it is my integrity at stake, their integrity is my integrity, their word is my word. If they see I am following through with their actions they will understand it is not just about setting the task, it is seeing it through and they will understand their actions, however small, have an impact in this world and that is empowering for them. You will feel good, they will feel good, there is direction and clarity in the relationship we have together. It shows we care enough about them, that we support them achieving the things they set out to do. If we are only ever asking when people set themselves tasks and not the follow through, then this is just lip service. Fulfilling relationships are created in the follow through.

"*Even when benefits for change are indisputable, we are geniuses at inventing reasons to avoid change.*" Marshall Goldsmith

"*Where there's a will, a Way will always be Made, Discovered, Found, or Created.*" Lucy Johnson, Fully Booked Formula

_____
_____
_____
_____
_____
_____

QUALITIES THAT STICKING TO WHAT YOU SAY DEVELOPS AND SUGGESTED ROLE MODELS: These men and women have such a strong sense of their compass and are at the source of themselves, they can very clearly understand what can affect them and others. They have a huge strength of character and demonstrate the multi-layeredness of living a fulfilling life. They really care about people and themselves, enough to speak out and say the hard things. They are up to big things and not afraid to roll up their sleeves, knuckle down and get on with what needs doing. They are my compassion warriors, they have the adept skill of being able to say anything to anyone because it comes from a place of love.

Below are examples of people I truly respect for their demonstration of STICKING TO WHAT THEY SAY THEY ARE GOING TO DO:

Brene Brown
Danielle la Porte
Gabrielle Bernstein
Susan David
David Goggins

"*#1: Know what you're seeking.*

#2: Set trigger goals.

#3: Set improvement goals.

#4: Gather a tribe.

#5: Script your setbacks. Anticipate how you'll feel and react ahead of time."
Tod Herman and Marie Forleo

"*Perseverance is the hard work you do after you get tired of doing the hard work you already did.*" Newt Gingrich

"*I don't divide the world into the weak and the strong. I divide the world into the learners and non-learners.*" Benjamin Barber

How you'd know when it's present?

☐ You will not be so affected by stress and you don't waste time on what could have been as you focus on the positives

☐ You choose to navigate through any upheavals or obstacles to your plans by being receptive to change or having a plan b

☐ You do not place too much weight on the present moment as you know things are likely to change and so hold to your original plan, unless there is good enough reason not to

☐ You are always listening to the advice of mentors who are more skilled than you at sticking to what they say they are going to do

☐ You are able to stick to what you say you will do without receiving others' approval and consistently acknowledge your small wins no matter how small

☐ You are extremely proud of yourself and not in an egotistical way as you know this creates a space for others to acknowledge themselves too

☐ With important actions you turn down the short-term gratification for the longer-term reward and are also human enough to realise you will give up, mess up and can forgive yourself to allow you to 'get back on the horse'

"Be passionate about the problem that you're solving. Overnight success is possible and don't be surprised if it takes years." Jon Lee, Founder Rabbut

"Keep your eyes on the stars and your feet on the ground." Teddy Roosevelt

How you'd know when it's not present?

☐ You are constantly stressed out by too many commitments. You feel empty and lost at times

☐ When negative things happen you are stopped in your tracks and cannot continue with your actions, you want to give up sometimes

☐ Things are too hard and you don't have a compelling enough reason to want to 'Stick at it', why should you, there are no consequences are there? Apart from your self-worth that is

☐ You do not listen to any advice unless it is something that boasts your ego or agrees with how you feel-'yes' friends

☐ You are addicted to constant motivational resources and rewards and still find it impossible to finish a lot of things

☐ You base your happiness on superficial rewards, never feel like 'you're there yet' and hardly ever feel fulfilled or satisfied

☐ You always put your needs first even if it means giving up on projects that you said you'd complete

"*Vision will get you inspired. Discipline will take you there.*" Christine Caine

"*Always do your best. What you plant now you will harvest later.*" Og Mandino

Daily Calibration Tool:

Why do some of us find it hard to STICK to something we say we are going to do? It can be a combination of many things ranging from, lack of accountability, lack of willpower, lack of consequences, lack of good role models around you or people to hold you to what you'd said. It's the hardest thing sometimes in the world to hold people to their word. We generally want to be popular and not have to make someone feel bad, but the good friends will do this

and you will appreciate it after some thinking about it.

However, for the most of everyday life it is down to us to run our lives and we will generally be aware of what we want to achieve and what is outstanding on our TO DO LIST. When we stop achieving things it is usually because we are afraid or overwhelmed by TOO MUCH TO DO and then getting back ON TRACK becomes too much hassle or just too overwhelming.

So we leave it like the proverbial bags of charity clothes that are sitting in the spare room for years, waiting to go to the shop. So what do we do to get the TO DO LIST smashed? We daily appreciate what we have as this puts us into a positive frame of mind where it is so much easier to get into action; combined with acknowledging the daily small steps. If we don't CHUNK down the achievements the large goals will remain TOO big and WAYYY too scary… Draw yourself out a Daily Appreciation Acknowledgement Chart today - then fill this in in the morning or evening, you choose!

"It does not matter how slowly you go as long as you do not stop." Confucius

"You don't have to wait for something 'meaningful' to come into your life so that you can finally enjoy what you do. There is more meaning in joy than you will ever need." Eckhart Tolle

"The universe doesn't hear what you say it hears what you mean." Abraham Hicks

"Even the sharp shooters among us have to be reminded to be happy. Mainly because we lack the structure to execute ambitions, and it's easier to scapegoat our environment." Marshall Goldsmith

"The person you are today is not the person who will achieve your goal." Marshall Goldsmith

_____
_____
_____
_____
_____
_____
_____

"*Confidence isn't an assuredness, it's a willingness to try.*" Mel Robbins

"*I pay a woman to call me every day to ask me questions on what I achieved yesterday with my behaviour goals - people ask me, why do I pay a woman when I'm teaching people to have guaranteed leadership growth - I WROTE the theory of how to change behaviour that's why I pay a woman to call me every day.*" Marshall Goldsmith

What changes will you make after reading this chapter?:

PASSION

Chapter 5

INDEX

When something's not working try something different

INDEX - when something's not working try something different

Definition:

This is about beliefs, conditioning and triggers - the 'Rules' we play by, but not necessarily the rules we wrote or initially agreed to. We are stuck in a habit loop of reactions: prove, protect, hide, defend, blame. Masters are acutely aware and practice using a different lens to view an environment where forgiveness, acceptance, celebration (Lisa Nichols), creation and commitment are possible.

"*Happiness is when the events of life meet your expectations of how you think life should be.*" Mo Gawdat, Happiness Equation.

"*The ego mind is not happy with - it's enough I'm alive. Yet the material world only brings temporary happiness.*" Marianne Williamson

Why is it beneficial?:

This is different to the others because you will not always have power, authenticity, being able to say what you will do, stick to what you say, obstacles and navigation present in your life. However you will always have an INDEX there because if there is a space it will always get filled; i.e. even if you try to not have a point of view, judgement or opinion one will always appear, because the human brain will keep a record of a situation and how it made you feel based on your values that were given to you from the environment you grew up in. This can be very useful when dealing with situations which may pose a risk to your survival and you need to have quick access to memories where you can reference your past decision and ask- 'did this pose a threat to me previously and what was the action I took?' However, we do not live in a society where there is immediate threat to our survival and this form of judgement can limit our viewpoint in which we see the world. So with a brain that is capable of making decisions for us we have to practice becoming mindful to our thoughts and the new lens that we wish to look at the world through. When practicing this it allows us to become aware when we are not being accepting of ourselves or others and willing to listen and understand better. This type of behaviour transforms situations and relationships and creates a type of trust that opens up our creative brain to opportunities that we couldn't have ever imagined.

"*If there's no change in meaning there's no healing.*" Donny Epstein

"*A good life is not a place in which you arise it's a lens through which you see and create your world. We want the destination vs the VIEWPOINT.*" Jonathan Fields

_____
_____
_____
_____
_____
_____

My journey with Index:

DECISION MAKING: INDEX is in every breath we take, every look we make, every feeling we have. It is there without us having to even think about it. It has become a subconscious, autonomous reaction, a habit loop of feelings. It's our set reactions you constantly hear from experts that we're defined by by the age of seven years old. In essence it is the brain connections that have been fused together to create the complex network of reactions and decisions you will always make when faced with a certain situation or person. This is our survival toolkit. Now in a period of relative stability and safety, the social world is now becoming more aware of subjects such as neuroscience, psychology, philosophy and emotional intelligence. We now have the luxury of understanding why we do what we do and want to make better decisions to create a better life, making a difference with what we do.

This sounds great and the evidence of millions of personal development books available online and thousands of training courses attended, shows we have certainly been giving this one a good go. Throughout time, wise authors have spoken about becoming aware and responsible for how we respond to things. You only have to take a look at the greek philosophers to see this delaying a response between our thinking and action was evident within the philosophical community thousands of years ago, so why does is seem like we are only just covering this topic now? There could be many reasons including, the subject of being responsible for our reactions is only of interest for a small minority, there is not enough evidence for the benefits of focusing on this or you cannot create an awareness where someone does not want to be aware.

I was never aware of my reactions and decision making till my late 30s and interestingly, your frontal cortex which is your executive reasoning centre in the brain, doesn't activate till your early 30s. All I know is that I lived my life for a couple of decades in a small bubble and still live in a reasonably small bubble as I haven't travelled as much as I would like or have read as much as I could have to understand things from many other perspectives. Daily, the more I practice becoming aware of my set INDEX, how I am conditioned to react and what I value, the more I can catch the emotion and deal with it.

What my INDEX 'in action' looks like in reality is having a very determined, serious and sometimes territorially aggressive approach to every action I do. I will drive as fast as I am legally able to, walk quickly past people, not want to stop and talk for long, keep my head down when doing a task or working and generally always being prepared to 'attack' if called for. This isn't conducive to having the best affect on people around me, and would likely lead to people feeling uncomfortable, in the way and not cared for. Obviously this is not the intention. I have two passions, interestingly diametrically opposed, I am an adrenaline based person and thrive on challenge but also love caring for the people around me. So when I began looking at some of my programmed reactions I felt they were not serving my key intentions of looking after people and ultimately myself.

"*Emotions, we either bottle them, push aside or fixate; rather than just open our heart to the full range of emotions. They are there as signposts for us to work through, there is no fix! We over-glamourise happiness in society, which takes us actually further away from happiness.*" Susan David

"*25% of success is down to intellect or skills. The rest is optimism, social skills and how we react to stress. Stress is a very important indicator in life and IS inevitable, we all go through it, the difference comes with the way people perceive it. In studies the people who positively saw stress, saw a 23% improvement in fatigue, back aches, headaches and a 31% increase in productivity and happiness.*" Shawn Achor

DEALING WITH CHALLENGE: Now I hang back in traffic as I would like to be more considerate to my passengers and other drivers, I am not so worried about cars cutting me up, I don't need to beep my horn, I do not need to react to a threat, nor prove it was their fault. I will pause if someone pushes past or says to me something cutting, they could be having a bad day or maybe a hard time. This literally only just happened a minute ago whilst writing this chapter, where I came out of the toilets and a lady pushed past me and didn't even say thank you for me holding the door open. I actually said under my breath, 'rude' but then realised this was a scared reaction from me that I felt threatened by her behaviour and that she didn't make me feel good by saying thank you back. A small example of a lack of courtesy and really minor compared to how some people treat other people without realising. But is it going to get any of us anywhere by confronting people and getting them to see the error of their ways because this is only our rules they have broken. When we are scared and confronted we will most of the time defend ourselves, it's a natural human reaction. The term 'road rage' is perhaps a phenomenon we have always experienced but just called it something different, in the past we might have encountered this as challenging someone to a dual.

"Never wish your life were easier, wish that you were better" Jim Rohn

"We're so full-up of what we know…Let go of what you know. Soften your focus and become present to what's there." Laura Whitworth

RELATIONSHIP TO THE EXTERNAL WORLD: Using the reference from the previous paragraph, a better way of handling this, when it is something worth saying, is explaining how it made us feel but not finger pointing, then at least it gives the other person the opportunity to see what happened from our perspective. They could then share that they were bursting for the toilet, had someone waiting for them and didn't mean to seem dismissive. Actually her dismissive behaviour is possibly how I act when I am not aware and single-mindedly going about my tasks and perhaps how I make others feel.

To use the electrons analogy of a circuit board - electrons are negatively charged and attracted to the positive end of a battery and repelled by the negative end. So we can only react to something we are not at peace with (negative charge) and the forceful drive I had as a child came from a reaction to respond to someone else's forceful drive (negative charge). When we close the loop and see where we are reacting to old circumstances (negative charge) the electron no longer finds negative charges to react to and now only sees the positive in everything. The electric current is then able to flow naturally without any resistance.

"*A problem is a chance for you to do your best.*" Duke Ellington.

"*JFK said 'ask not what your country can do for you, but what you can do for your country.' I would take that even further, companies should be asking what are you going to do for them with no expectancy of them returning anything. Companies are not in charge of your engagement, this is clear when you look at two air stewards on the same flight, same uniform, same rules, same engagement package, yet one is happy and one is miserable. When you're a coach pick the ones that want to improve their situation and don't make it about you.*" Marshall Goldsmith

QUALITIES THAT BEING AWARE OF INDEX DEVELOPS and SUGGESTED ROLE MODELS:
I think from the example above, being aware of your INDEX helps you become better at your understanding of physics and circuitry! Joking aside, it is all chain reactions and the best role models are committed to practicing being patient and considerate, brave enough to question their responses and listen to others and what is going on in their worlds. The people below are specialists in compassion, stoicism, emotional intelligence and personal development. As Mark Manson says 'my favourite moments are when something bitchslaps my brain and reconfigures my entire understanding of reality and my place within it.'

Below are examples of people I truly respect for their demonstration of BEING AWARE OF THEIR INDEX:

Brene Brown
Ryan Holiday
Dr Alan Watkins
Mark Manson
Viktor Frankl

"*He that is good with a hammer tends to think everything is a nail.*" Abraham Maslow

"*Genes require input from the environment to work properly. It's not always the people who start out the smartest, end up the smartest.*" Carol Dweck

"*Everybody is a genius. But if you judge a fish by its ability to climb a tree, it will live its whole life believing that it is stupid.*" Albert Einstein

How you'd know when you're aware?

☐ You are more able to understand decisions made by others and can put yourself in their shoes

☐ When something negative happens you are able to objectify it and look from an outsider's point of view, what's happening in their world?

☐ You look at the present moment through yours and other people's lenses and are curious not controlling

☐ You are very aware of the different ways people react to their world and allow for this, but communicate any unmet expectations

☐ You appreciate others but do not automatically expect them to appreciate you back, it is enough you appreciate you

☐ You are responsible for yourself, your environment and your impact on people. You do this not to impress but out of a commitment to be the best version of you

☐ You are not afraid to 'put yourself at stake', i.e. look at yourself from an external perspective and ask, could I have done better, but more importantly what can I acknowledge myself for?

"We think we understand the rules when we become adults, but what we really experience is a narrowing of the imagination." David Lynch

"I don't believe in age. I believe in energy. Don't let age dictate what you can and cannot do." Tao Porchon-Lynch 97-year-old yoga teacher

How you'd know when you're not aware?

☐ You struggle to understand why people say and do what they do and feel hurt a lot by circumstances

☐ When negative things happen you are highly reactive and respond 100% from your viewpoint of how it made you feel

☐ You allow your feelings to overtake the present moment and are consumed by constant judgements and over-analysis

☐ You are not interested in learning about what makes a difference to others only that they understand you and what you want

☐ You demand respect first before you give it. Yet cannot understand why if you don't trust others why they can't trust you back

☐ You are always reacting to triggers/stimuli in the environment and not at the source of your results

☐ You are always desperate to prove yourself and want to feel vindicated in your actions. There is an externalness (how you feel about yourself is linked to the outside world) about you, rather than 'being with' who you are

"If you are holding something in your life that you do not like, let it go. With your hands open, you will be able to grab hold of something new. Whether it is a fish, a person, a deal, or just a moment in time, your life can be steered in the direction you want as long as your feet are in one boat." Suze Orman

"The mind is its own place, and in itself can make a heaven of hell and a hell of heaven..."
Milton

"'A Battle Between Two Wolves' - The grandfather explains to his grandchild, one wolf is full of hate and one is full of happiness. The child asks, which wolf will win? The grandfather replies, the one you feed." An old Cherokee legend

Daily Calibration Tool:

INDEX is all about the constraints of our past and moving beyond them through:

1/ becoming aware of what they are

2/ and having some very useful tools to support new actions and goals

With this in mind, it is a great idea to GET OUTSIDE of OURSELVES and go seek NEW SITUATIONS, PEOPLE and OPPORTUNITIES.

However, this will not be easy as it will mean CHANGING our BEHAVIOUR and thus making us feel UNCOMFORTABLE. Some suggested tasks you can do to change your INDEX are:

1/ Find new situations that STRETCH you with PEOPLE that are BETTER than you at what it is you seek to become; i.e. Conferences, Exhibitions, Courses, Seminars in the specific subject area you seek awareness in

2/ Look for or research new ROLE MODELS that are masters at your goals

3/ Write down where you might have been STOPPED previously and WHY that might have been. What new ACTION could you now take:

- Dump and change it
- Go for it again
- Recreate something better

Basically go LIVE IN THE ZONE, if it feels uncomfortable, then it's generally working.

"*It's not about the goal, it's about how you want to feel when you get there.*" *Danielle la Porte*

"*We are not supposed to come through this life perfectly! It's NEEDING people and being needed!*" *Glennon Doyle Melton*

What changes will you make after reading this chapter?:

_____
_____
_____
_____
_____
_____
_____
_____
_____
_____
_____
_____

PASSI**O**N

Chapter 6

OBSTACLES

Love the imperfections

OBSTACLES Love the imperfections

Definition:
You will 100% be defeated by negative self-talk at many points in your life. We can't be with ourselves and our shame, scarcity, comparison transfers in our conversations and relationships. Masters learn compassion and empathy, always.

"*5 things we do that make us unhappy: Control, Compare, Hate Mistakes, Ignore Your Friends, Surround yourself with negative.*" Lilly Singh, Superwoman

"*If you feel great, then not, that's part of life, you learn through contrast. So then just say, Stop! I don't want to serve the monkey mind.*" Danielle la Porte

Why is it beneficial?:

'Negative self-talk' isn't beneficial at all, however, being aware of our negative self-talk is very useful and definitely a daily tool we can utilise - actions to practice are captured below in the daily calibration section. Our negative self-talk is all-consuming. Eckhart Tolle who is mentioned in this book, talks about the ego as separate to our consciousness. There are two of us in our brain or else we wouldn't be able to question ourselves like we do. Most of the time we get stuck in our heads for too long, in deep self-analysis and for most of this, this is the ego brain. It is only when we stop our incessant thinking and 'notice' our thoughts - we become our consciousness and just let them roll without having an opinion on them or be drawn into concern for them and what they could or couldn't mean. This type of activity is called meditation and it allows us to stop the over-analysis and 're-set' our brains back to neutral. Once we can practice this more often it means we can let go of a lot of negativity or bad thoughts about ourselves and become a lot more proactive than reactive. The less being stuck in our thoughts also means we can listen more to others - how often I find myself having trailed off in my own thoughts, only one sentence after someone has started talking. We can also be a lot more compassionate when we are less harsh on ourselves.

"Real knowledge is to know the extent of one's ignorance." Mo Gawdat speaking at WBECS

"Social Media - a weapon of mass destruction to our self-esteem." Iskra Lawrence

My journey with Obstacles:

DECISION MAKING: When I am teaching the PASSION tools to new students and start the section on OBSTACLES I always say this should be OBSTACLE as there is only one. And that, as you can probably guess, is yourself. You've probably heard this said, that you can be your own best friend and own worst enemy all at the same time; and actually the trick to most business success is getting yourself out of your own way. We all too often create barriers that are not there, which usually come from limiting beliefs about ourselves and others.

When I first did my Coaching Diploma I threw myself into the limiting beliefs section in the hope that it could 'cure' me of all my limitations in life just like a magic wand. Personal development isn't about reading a few books and then you solve the mystery. It takes a lot of listening to role models, applying actions and then repeating. What I also found was I'm not a big advocate of beliefs and affirmations. This is because no matter how much I looked myself in the mirror and said positive phrases it didn't change a single thing about how I really felt about myself. It felt fake and misguided. I am sure affirmations and vision boards work really well for some people, just not me. What I discovered is that I am a student of behavioural re-programming, I saw the positive results in taking daily actions and making decisions that pushed me out of my comfort zone and which saw me slowly behave myself into believing anything was possible.

"*Beliefs are great but if you have an opposing non-conscious belief, then you just won't do it. The brain is an organ that we are just getting hold of the manual.*" John Assaraf

DEALING WITH CHALLENGE: When wanting to make consistent progress in the face of daily life and circumstances the three key focuses for me which I have taken from Tony Robbin's work are:

1/ Set up your physiology for a successful day 2/ Have great role models 3/ Focus on something other than yourself.

1/ Setting up your physiology is about changing your mental state and your patterns. Fear is physical and if you do something physical you are more likely to interrupt that state of fear. Tony Robbins does this through swearing and shouting at people and making them laugh. Wim Hof does this through deep breathing techniques to create low carbon dioxide levels in the blood which lead to higher alkalinity and even having an impact on psychological processes. He also swims in freezing cold water and runs through boiling hot deserts. So think of something new today that's physical that will allow you to challenge some of your negative self-talk.

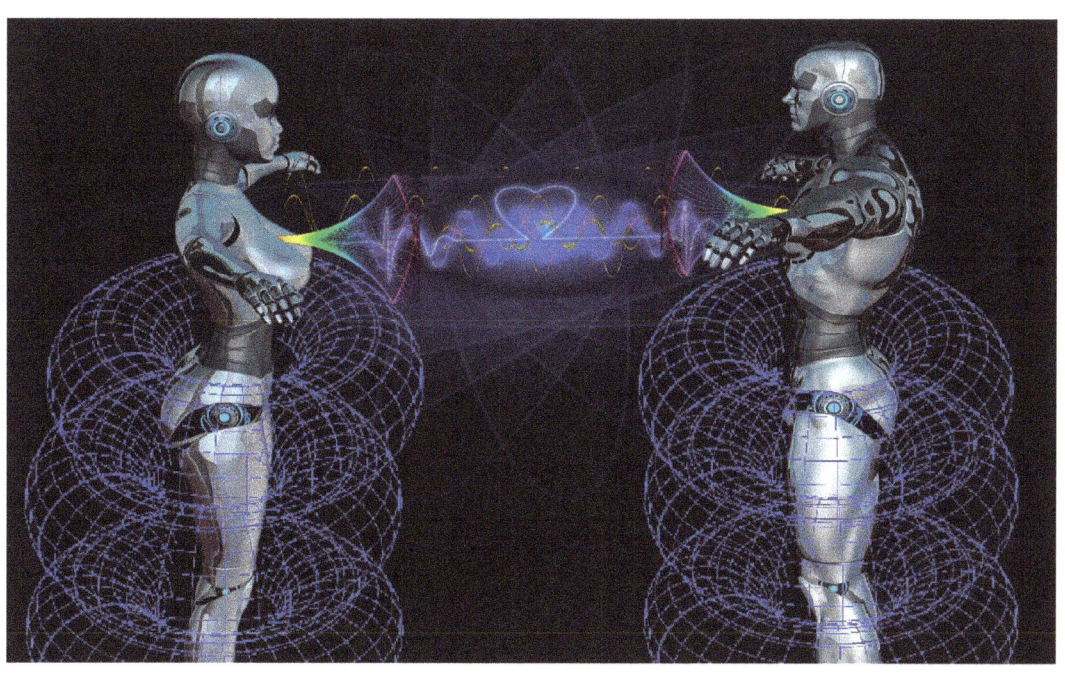

> "ADVANCE TOWARDS FEAR - as you face that you then are able to ADVANCE TOWARDS FREEDOM - which then gives you a new lens that you are powerful and have ADVANCED TO FULFILMENT." David Vobora interviewed by Lewis Howes

> "Everything resonates on an energy level 200-1000 (Hertz vibrational frequency). If you are below 200 you will take on negative energy, for example a baby crying is around 160 so a mother takes it in her arms and soothes with the kindness of her breast. I'm 62 and I know three hours of that would soothe me too!" Wayne Dyer

RELATIONSHIP TO THE EXTERNAL WORLD: Continuing Tony Robbins Key Focuses:

2/ Role models are so vital because they allow us to challenge our current thinking with the thinking of someone who has lived and breathed what we have set ourselves as a goal, who we want to be and how we want to live our life. I've heard it said that never take criticism off someone who has not achieved what you are trying to achieve. Recently I have seen how important great role models are with my own current mentor. Plus I have also seen the importance of establishing the right role model for you. Just because they are successful doesn't mean they have the relevant experience or indeed advice for you. Trust your gut and if you are being advised and don't believe it represents what it is you are trying to achieve or the person doesn't align with your expectations, then move on. Also see how you can start to become a role model - see the daily calibration tool for OBSTACLES - on mapping yours and others' emotional experience and where we all are in the galaxy of 34,000 emotions.

3/ Focusing on something other than myself has been the mechanism for me getting out of my own way. I can be at times a very intense person and uncontrollably analytical. When I first started practicing acknowledging something daily and appreciating something or someone in my daily routine, I found this very tedious and at times hard to identify. The more I practiced it, I could slowly see myself becoming a lot more aware about the many things in my life that I had to be grateful for; and even more gradually the things I did that I could acknowledge myself for. It would get to the point where in the middle of the day, small insignificant things would be occurring to me, like I'm so lucky I managed to get my shopping done before the store closed and that I have a nice warm car to get me home. Even to the point where I'm in the main bathroom in my house and looking at the silvery glitter carpet I had fitted last year and just thinking how much that carpet makes me happy to look at every day. This may seem absurd but I am a lot more appreciative for my life and a lot happier with what I've achieved. This year when completing 2018 and planning 2019 I was for the first time properly proud of myself and could actually concede there had been progress - yes concede! When I look up concede in Wikipedia it says: deny, resist, surrender, yield - this is exactly what happened to me, my negative self-talk denied me self-acknowledgment for so long and now I have been able to surrender because of my daily practice. I also practice smiling at everyone I pass by and make a promise to pick up some litter on every walk I go on. I'm pretty sure I could make these actions a lot more bodacious - I have a vision of buying an old container ship and picking up litter in the ocean. I think the PASSION Toolset as a book is a great start for all of us to collectively focus on something other than ourselves.

"*Many people think that pain is bad. Pain is a mandatory part of life. And sometimes it is a reminder we should change.*" *Marshall Goldsmith*

_____
_____
_____
_____
_____

"I guarantee there have been significant learning takeaways that have melded you into who you are today as an entrepreneur and as an individual. Save those moments. When you're in a 'valley,' refer back to those instances to summit the next peak." Jeff Boss, entrepreneur

QUALITIES THAT DEALING WITH OBSTACLES DEVELOPS AND SUGGESTED ROLE MODELS: These people are excellent at getting themselves out of their own way. They give so much practical advice in dealing with some complex subjects such as ego, presence and consciousness, meditation, societal conditioning, behaviour and spirituality. If there's one thing they would all say it would probably be adapt or die. We have to understand our limitations but then have the strength to move past it and that resilience can also sometimes be about breaking. We are not supposed to get through this perfectly, it's about supporting each other and being honest about where we can't do it all.

Below are examples of people I truly respect for their demonstration of DEALING WITH OBSTACLES:

Tony Robbins
Eckhart Tolle
Seth Goddin
Wayne Dyer
Abraham Hicks
Caroline Myss

"We beat ourselves up thinking that we're doing something wrong because we don't seem to be moving as quickly as we perceive others are." Marie Forleo

"What makes us joyful = our capacity to give ourselves fully to the world and receive a richness of experience available every moment." Henry Kimsey-House

"You're drowning in mental stuff, for ten, twenty, forty years, what kind of habitual consciousness does that produce, what kind of person?" Eckhart Tolle

"*Seemingly benign environments with small deviations are actually when we need to be alert. We don't need to learn what to do but what to avoid.*" Peter Drucker

"*All of the magic in your personal life happens when you rush towards the pain instead of away from it. ...what would be available if we rushed toward the pain of the world? It's not about healing ourselves completely before we heal the world.*" Glennon Doyle Melton

How you'd know when you're dealing with it?

☐ You practice a form of meditation or being with your thoughts, letting them go and giving yourself space

☐ You can be with your negative thoughts as you know they are not who you are and at any time you can turn things around

☐ You are able to use negative situations to your favour, i.e. you take what has happened and see how you can learn from it/ do better/ become stronger

☐ You never allow others' negativity to impact you, and at times remove toxic people and situations from your world

☐ You consistently look to feed your inner-self with 'good energy' from sources that are important to you

☐ You are more present than most people, having 'considered responses' and a more centred state in any situation

☐ You are not afraid to put your inner-self work as a priority as you know it will mean you can focus on others a lot more, once the distractions have been dispelled

"*Social connection is a greatest predictor of long-term happiness and therefore increased business profit. Build a two minute habit of thanking people in your workforce/ life.*" Shawn Achor

"*What a liberation to realise that the 'voice in my head' is not who I am. Who am I then? The one who sees that.*" Eckhart Tolle

"We get clarity then we muck it all up with self-judgement.. FREEZE FRAME!.. You want what you want, you might not get it, but denying it won't get you anywhere better." Feelings first! Don't just oommm your way to a state- take some life-affirming actions that forward the feelings you long for." Danielle la Porte

How you'd know when you're not dealing with it?

- ☐ You are stuck in your thoughts and feel overwhelmed to the point of feeling stressed and anxious a lot of the time
- ☐ You cannot be with negative things without feeling pity, shame or guilt and this transfers to your conversation with others
- ☐ You cannot be in the present moment; you are always worrying about past mistakes or a future of change, risk, or uncertainty
- ☐ You allow others' negativity to impact your thoughts and stay too long in situations that drag you and your positivity down
- ☐ You do not prioritise working on yourself 'inside' and only look to external quick fixes, ending up feeling tired of life
- ☐ You appear constantly distracted, harassed and overwhelmed by even the smallest events
- ☐ You don't know how to do the work on yourself and are unaware of the negative self-talk; or possibly don't care what this is and the implications

"It's ok to go down those dead-end roads but it's not ok to get stuck there because the only person we're harming is ourselves." Cheryl Strayed

"Regards the big question of 'just give me more time!' It's not true.. Leonardo da Vinci never had twenty six hours in a day. Even if we had two more hours, it would be two more hours of overwhelm and stickiness.. Psychological bandwidth is what is needed.. The ability to clear the fuzziness and control and focus on the right things.. It's simple but not easy!!" David Allen, Productivity coach

"We never lose our demons, we only learn to live above them." by The Ancient One, Doctor Strange Film

Daily Calibration Tool:

With an interest in Personal Development you will know that our only real OBSTACLE is OURSELVES. However, when in the darkest moments or when feeling a failure it is useless just to say, 'oh pull yourself together, it is only your negative self-talk!' So as you may also know it is practicing becoming aware when we get TOO MUCH IN OUR HEAD and show ourselves a bit of softness and compassion before we push it aside. Please look up Dr Alan Watkins who is an expert in the study of the impact of emotions on our neuro-psychology. In the meantime:

1/ Capture your emotions that stop you, as they occur. Practice looking from the outside, don't be consumed by your emotions

2/ Start writing down and characterising your emotions with more descriptive words and phrases. This will allow you to record in more detail what could be stopping you and allow you to let it go when you fully understand it

3/ Catch the negative emotion like a tennis ball and then throw it away. This is a physical action and fear is also physical, so these tangible movements are allowing us to grasp and deal with what have been intangible emotions till this point

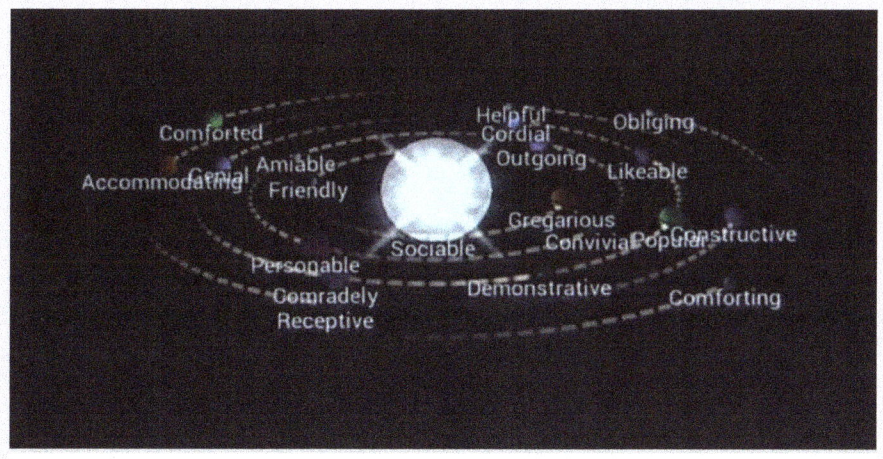

My Pocket Coach
October 10, 2017

"If you're lucky you have a crisis in your life where you question the "rules" then it becomes the disease of meaning. So to blot out the pain that I can't answer the question of life I use either anaesthetics or physical, material, or work addiction. Because we think the solution is outside of ourselves. It's about looking at your own emotional experience. The e-motions (energy of body's processes) are always there but we haven't learnt to process them. Most of us don't know where we are in the galaxy of 34,000 emotions and therefore have no control. Let alone able to map who's on planet "social" or "disgruntled". And once you get to a more effective planet system, can you stay there? You will need to take a subjective emotion and "objectify" it, ask what is my anger?

WHY IMPORTANT TO UNDERSTAND THIS:

Emotions - predict your Health/Well-being/Fulfilment/ Ability to make Decisions

One Q

What planet do you want to spend your time on?"

Dr Alan Watkins Neuroscientist, @CCoherence

"Happiness is like a butterfly. The more you chase it, the more it will elude you, but if you turn your attention to other things, it will come and sit softly on your shoulder."
Nathaniel Hawthorne

"When you structure a pitch (and daily life for that matter), you don't need motivation. Most importantly understand the value you bring - it's not about money, money is everywhere, you're the prize."
Oren Klaff @PitchAnything

"People think I'm done with this crap job, one day I can live my dreams, NO this now is the gateway to your dreams, you do your job now to the best, become a master at that, and that fuels the next level."
Dean Graziosi

"When you realise how perfect everything is you will tilt your head back and laugh at the sky" Buddha

"A lot of Personal Development does bring about an obsession with ourselves - we need 'Outrospection' as opposed to Introspection. This is created by practising empathy."
YourBrainHealth.com.au Dr Sarah McKay PhD

"*Shame is imagined, there is no shame in anything, it is just fear in disguise, once we are honest about it, it disappears.*" Glennon Doyle Melton

"*The wound is the place where the light enters you.*" Rumi

What changes will you make after reading this chapter?:

PASSIO**N**

Chapter 7

NAVIGATION

Practice, practice, practice

NAVIGATION - practice, practice, practice

Definition:
Daily habits create OR undo our aspirations and direct our business culture. Masters stay awake and/or measure and/or successfully control the small bad psychological habits that keep us below our potential.

"We don't rise to the level of our expectations, we default to the level of our training."
Richard Marcinko, Seal Team 6

"The more you learn to create successful daily rituals/ systems/ processes- to activate your emotional centres and motivational behaviours, i.e. how you start the day, deal with stress, plan, evaluate, follow through - puts you in a cycle of success - then the easier it becomes to achieve success." John Assaraf

Why is it beneficial?:

We've probably all heard the saying, 'if you don't know where you're going, how will you know when you've got there?' Like a lot of the things I discuss in this book, this is a seemingly obvious requirement of living an effective life but how many of us actually have a clear plan we stick to, or consistently review? It actually takes very little time, maybe a few hours, to review a previous year and state your goals for the next year, but why is it something we mostly avoid? It could be that accountability is harder to do when you are holding yourself to account because you forget to check-in, but also when we put things in writing any failures will be visible. Whereas if we haven't said we'd do it, we do not consider it a failure. So there are many benefits to having a NAVIGATION system in your life, including: achieving goals that we did not think possible, a feeling of aliveness when we do, even the feeling when we have failed is still that of a person who is in action; plus the feeling of self-esteem as you know you are giving 100% effort. You also positively benefit other people's worlds because you are clearly communicating to everyone you work and live with and so people know where they are with you and as a result enjoy being around you.

"The secret to success is the uncommon application of common practices." Ivan Misner

"When your child starts to love learning, or you and your spouse start communicating better, the problem doesn't go away. These changes have to be supported or they can go away quicker than they appear." Carol Dweck

"We are what we repeatedly do. Excellence, then, is not an act, but a habit." Aristotle

"*Radar speed displays show feedback loops work - action/ information/ reaction and have been shown to decrease speeding by 30-60%.*" Marshall Goldsmith

"*What gets measured, gets improved.*" Peter Drucker

My journey with Navigation:

DECISION MAKING: NAVIGATION has always been my favourite tool of the PASSION Toolset. This is because it is where change and transformation actually happen. The discipline of actually setting even one small behavioural task edges you towards that goal or even breaking through a mental block. High performing habits create aspirations and low performing ones undo your aspirations. Previously a lot of the time I would take copious amounts of action and I would still feel I was getting nowhere. Mainly because I was unclear what my offering to the market was or what I wanted in exchange. This is the same with any new goal or behaviour. It takes a lot of actions, failing and trying new things to discover how to get good at your new goal or if people will be willing to pay for a service or product. The key is to set new measures and then reassess regularly what is and isn't working. See the Daily Calibration Tool for Navigation later on in this chapter. This is the readjustment part of NAVIGATION. When recalibrating you need to be aware of two things when taking new actions 1/ will this make the boat go faster i.e. provide something that will be competitive and valuable? 2/ how much is this going to stretch my breaking point - challenge me to become better and fulfill me?

"Structure not only increases our chances of success it makes us more efficient at it"
Marshall Goldsmith

"When we dive 100% into adult behavioural change, we change our environment, we have become the trigger." *Marshall Goldsmith*

DEALING WITH CHALLENGE: The key thing is to just stay awake. This actually is not easy as life does happen and we have to remember every minute to take back life. This can either be through a series of reminders we set or habits we build: that allow us to use important moments each day to breathe before saying anything, or even in a moment where we are going off track, train ourselves to recognise that these actions are not serving any other purpose than being distractions. It is also about seeing those small bad psychological habits for what they are. For me this was spending a lot of time on social media and dating sites. I felt my energy was being dragged down by using a dating site as it never seemed to make me feel good about myself. There were a lot of short conversations that never went anywhere and before I knew it, two hours of my evening had gone. Now with my phone time, I put my phone out of the way for most of the day when I'm concentrating on work and have no phone time for an hour in the evening before I go to bed so I can completely relax and switch off. Another small bad psychological habit is not acknowledging my work or any wins and so to counter act this I have a very senior business industry mentor who pushes me to see everything I have achieved. Actually she champions me even to the point of being fiercely protective of any toxic people in my life.

"The distance between the one I am and the one I want to be, is what I do today." Sybille Greiner

RELATIONSHIP TO THE EXTERNAL WORLD: The sports coaches I've been fortuitous to have listened to in business seminars and podcasts have been some of the most inspiring in the way they NAVIGATE through living and performing in a highly competitive world. Michael Jordan was quoted as saying, "talent wins games, but teamwork and intelligence wins championships." This is why being able to intelligently set goals and respond to your environment is crucial for your success. Another key element touched on by Sir Clive Woodward is the way he deals with game analysis. On the days they lost a game in world championship rugby he would take his team down to the pub for celebrating what they had put into the game. On the days they won at their rugby game he would gather everyone round for a team meeting to discuss what had not worked or worked so well that they could take it forward for other games. This is an extremely resilient approach as it takes all of the emotion out of results and removes that association of winning as the only outcome. The last element Sir Clive talks about is this idea of it being one team and not being about theory. He advocates getting out there and doing it - share information - learn - input your knowledge. It's all about having the right attitude built on extraordinary habits, like Sir Clive's TCUP of Thinking Correctly Under Pressure.

The key thing that allows successful NAVIGATION is finding out how you get the right lessons learnt shared with a team or with the people in your world who support you moving forward.

"*Without a map, you are simply reacting to road signs and conditions. If my own journey taught me anything, it's that I didn't know what my goals and dreams were until I set a course and ended up hating where I arrived. Knowing what you don't want is as fruitful as knowing what you want. Where you are headed next? Torch your goals!*" Ashley Huffman

QUALITIES THAT NAVIGATION DEVELOPS AND SUGGESTED ROLE MODELS: These are the heroes, the peak performers, the guys who push the limits on what's physically and emotionally possible. They tell it the way it is and take no prisoners. They know it's not about necessarily liking everyone you play and work with, more about having a joint mission that you build strong relationships around. Leaders who NAVIGATE successfully understand that context is king and when you are able to get the very best out of your environment you can transform anything. True navigational leadership qualities are executing what you said and accepting that important decisions will be controversial which ultimately create a culture of trust where everyone feels free to disagree. A truly aspirational place - 'aspire' meaning 'breathe life into.' (Judith E. Glaser)

Below are examples of people I truly respect for their demonstration of NAVIGATIONAL ABILITY:

Sir Clive Woodward
Mark Foster
Jesse Itzler
Admiral McRaven
Wim Hof
Judith E. Glaser

Viktor Frankl's formula for a better life:

1/ Do good work.

2/ Experience beauty in some thing or some one.

3/ Attitude towards suffering ceases when find meaning.

How you'd know when it's present?

☐ You have a clear vision and communicate that with ease so that people understand you

☐ You know that when something negative happens that it is okay as you will stick to your navigation tools

☐ You are able to stick with the long-term plan and also pay attention to anything that appears in the present moment, choosing to deviate slightly if needs be

☐ You chose navigation for the very reason that you are aware of your impact on the outside world and can remain steady in the face of changing circumstances

☐ Your navigational plan gives you every confidence you could need and allows you to feel calm in the face of adversity

☐ You are disciplined and not afraid of hard work or failing; because no amount of success comes without falling first

☐ You know that having a plan, although hard to consistently stick to and may mean sacrificing time with others; along the way provides a lot of fulfilment and ability to improve with it

The four agreements, Don Miguel Ruez

- *I AM IMPECCABLE WITH MY WORD…*
- *I DON'T TAKE ANYTHING PERSONALLY. …*
- *I DON'T MAKE ASSUMPTIONS. …*
- *I ALWAYS DO MY BEST. …*
- *I LIVE IN THE NOW*

How you'd know when it's not present?

☐ You do not have a clear direction and because of this hesitate with making even the simplest decisions

☐ When negative things happen you react immediately with your first response and have no tools for dealing with this

☐ You let the present moment change your daily plans, and find that 'to-do-lists' become bigger with "urgent but not important" stuff taking precedence over "important but not urgent"

☐ You don't know how to respond to others when challenged over any plans or goals you may have and have no way of prioritising

☐ You constantly seek guidance and approval from any sources possible and don't show discernment over what you use as a guiding force

☐ You are afraid of failing and would prefer not to have to ask the hard questions of how to improve on anything

☐ You like other people's plans better than your own and prefer others' to make decisions for you; but you end up feeling directionless and bored

"In essence, if we want to direct our lives, we must take control of our consistent actions. It's not what we do once in awhile that shapes our lives, but what we do consistently."
Tony Robbins

"The Reciprocal Miracle is when we are both Aware AND Engaged - we positively impact another's environment by choosing to change our behaviour." Marshall Goldsmith

_____
_____
_____
_____
_____
_____
_____

"*Pushing yourself to the limits doesn't mean you are resilient, knowing how to keep the balance between working and resting does.*" Ana Erkic

Daily Calibration Tool:

The best NAVIGATION QUESTIONS I have seen to date and the ones I have pictured on my three-month family calendar board are:

Marshall Goldsmith's - SIX ACTIVE DAILY QUESTIONS - "Did I do my best to."

Marshall who is one of the world's leading executive coaches has someone call him daily to ask him these questions.

Six active questions
Did I do my best to:

- Be happy?
- Find meaning?
- Be fully engaged?
- Build positive relationships?
- Set clear goals?
- Make progress toward goal achievement?

"*I have to tick the boxes today for a great tomorrow, even when I don't feel like it. Focus on your day as: emotional, physical, creative and spiritual elements to be achieved.*" James Altucher

"*If you don't make time to work on creating the life you want, you're eventually going to be forced to spend a lot of time dealing with a life you don't want.*" Kevin Ngo

"*The trick is to enjoy life. Don't wish away your days, waiting for better ones ahead.*" Majorie Pay Hinckley

What changes will you make after reading this chapter?:

Bibliography

Author	Source/ Title	Date
Abraham, Jay	Advanced strategy of preeminence podcast.	15th Apr 2012
	The strategy of preeminence, understanding the needs of your clients podcast.	31st July 2015
	How to 10X your business with Lewis Howes podcast	29th Nov 2016
Achor, Shawn	"The happiness advantage" linking positive brains to performance at TEDx Bloomington.	30th Jun 2011
	The happy secret to better work at TEDx Bloomington.	1st Feb 2012
	"Before happiness", Talks at Google	10th Feb 2014.
Ali, Muhammed	Tweeting in February 2013 @MuhammadAli	Feb 2013
Allen, David	The art of stress-free productivity, TEDx Claremont colleges	30th Oct 2012
Altucher, James	How to reinvent yourself and create the future with Lewis Howes podcast	28th Dec 2016
Angelou, Maya	Angelou told Bill Moyers in a 1973 interview.	1973
Aristotle	Misattributed: Was actually Will Durant in The Story of Philosophy: The Lives and Opinions of the Greater Philosophers	1926
Assaraf, John	Unlocking your brains full potential with Lewis Howes podcast. www.myneurogym.com/brain-athon	31 Oct 2016.
Barber, Benjamin	The Reader's digest vol. 140, no. 837-842 (1992), p.159	1992
Barker, Eric	Decoding Myths of Success with Lewis Howes.	10th May 2017
Batiz, Suzy	The founder of Poo-Pourri used intuition to start a $300 million company, Marie Forleo podcast	10 Apr 2018
Benioff, Marc	Behind the Cloud: The untold story of how salesforce.com went from idea to Billion-Dollar Company-and revolutionized an industry	9th Nov 2009
Bernard Shaw George	George Bernard Shaw his life and works: a critical biography, Hurst and Blackett London	1911
Beswick, Cris	Building a Culture of Innovation, Bucharest Technology week.	4th Oct 2017
	The Truth of It Podcast	19th Mar 2018
Bond Chapman, Sandra	Make your brain smarter: increase your brain's creativity, energy and focus.	1st Jan 2013
	Make your brain smarter it's not what you think, TEDxRockcreekpark.	15th May 2013

	Brain blood flow and synchrony markers of neural health podcast.	25th June 2014
	Flex your cortex 7 secrets to turbocharge your brain TEDxBayArea.	19th Dec 2014
Boss, Jeff	Managing the mental game: how to think more effectively, navigate uncertainty and build mental fortitude	24th Nov 2016
Briggs, Myer	Myers Briggs questionnaire first established by Katharine Cook Briggs and Isabel Briggs Myers	1943
Broun, Heywood	Ames Daily Tribune, after his speech after he visited Ames	Jan 1974
Brown, Brene	The power of vulnerability TED talk.	3rd Jan 2011
	Listening to shame ted talk.	16th Mar 2012
	Why your critics aren't the ones who count, 99U podcast.	4th Dec 2013
	Daring greatly to unlock your creativity with Chase Jarvis podcast.	10th Apr 2014.
	Daring Classrooms, SXSWedu 2017 keynote.	7th Apr 2017.
	7 Super tips equalman podcast.	8th Aug 2017
	The Book Braving the wilderness: the quest for true belonging and the courage to stand alone.	12 Sept 2017
	Brene Brown shows you how to Brave the wilderness with Marie Forleo podcast.	12 Sept 2017
	Create true belonging and heal the world with Lewis Howes podcast.	13th Sept 2017
	Dr Brene Brown on transcending failure and rising strong, Oprah Supersoul Sunday.	19th Nov 2017
Brown, Derren	Sacrifice documentary, Netflix	2018
Buddha	Misattributed: (tilt head) Sounds like it could be a stanza from a Tibetan Dzoghcen text says George Draffan on www.fakebuddhaquotes.com: Since everything is but an illusion, Perfect in being what it is, Having nothing to do with good or bad, Acceptance or rejection, One might as well burst out laughing! This is from chapter 1 of "The Great Perfection's Self-Liberation in the Nature of Mind," by Longchenpa	(1308-1364)
Caine, Christine	Unstoppable: step into your purpose, run your race, embrace the future.	2018
Canfield, Jack	Chicken soup for the soul	28th June 1993
Cannon, Walter Bradford	In 1915, he coined the term fight or flight to describe an animal's response to threats in Bodily Changes in Pain, Hunger, Fear and Rage: An Account of Recent Researches into the Function of Emotional Excitement., and he expanded on Claude Bernard's concept of homeostasis.	1915
Carey, Jim	Starred in Yes Man, comedy film	2008

Cherokee Legend	The story of the Two Wolves is a popular 21st century legend of unknown origin, attributed to Native Americans, possibly Lenape or Cherokee or parable that is also known as "Which one do you feed", "Grandfather Tells", "The Wolves Within", and "Tale Of Two Wolves"	
Churchill, Winston	Churchill did say: "No one can guarantee success in war, but only deserve it." And he did say: "Success always demands a greater effort." Their Finest Hour, London: Cassell, page 434. Note to Robert Menzies, same volume, page 541.	1949
Collaut, Catherine	How to re-programme your subconscious mind to get what you want with Marie Forleo podcast	18th Sept 2012
Confucius	The Analects, The wisdom of Confucius 479 BC took 30-50 years to write,	1900
Confucius	The wisdom of Confucius	1900
Copp, Lynne	British institute of facilities management conference, speech Lynne Copp Worklife company	28th Jan 2013
Covey, Stephen R	The 7 habits of highly effective people. Stephen R Covey speaking at University of Pennsylvania podcast Freepress 1989.	19th Nov 2012
Daskal, Lolly	The leadership gap: what gets between you and your greatness	30th May 2017
David, Susan	The art of emotional agility with Lewis Howes podcast. The gift and power of emotional courage TED talks.	18th Feb 2018 20th Feb 2018
Derrickson, Spaihts, Cargill, Directors	The Ancient One, Doctor Strange film Film	Aired 2016
Donne, John	No man is an island may refer to: "No man is an island", a famous line from Devotions upon Emergent Occasions, a 1624 prose work by English poet John Donne	1624
Doyle Melton, Glennon	Broken is the beginning podcast. On being a Love Warrior interviewed by Marie Forleo TV. First the pain then the rising with Oprah Supersoul sessions.	11th Mar 2014 6th Sept 2016 10th May 2017.
Drucker, Peter	Michele Hunt interviews the iconic Peter Drucker on youtube. These 10 Peter Drucker quotes may change your world www.entrepreneur.com	28th Apr 2015 16th Sept 2014
Dweck, Carol	Mindset: the new psychology of success. How we can learn to fulfil our potential	2007

Dyer, Dr Wayne	Mastering the art of manifesting, Wanderlust's Speakeasy podcast.	19th Apr 2013
	How to attract what you want into your life, FoodForThought podcast.	8th Sept 2013
	Dr Wayne Dyer interview with Tony Robbins.	31st Aug 2015.
Dyrdek, Rob	On building a media empire with Lewis Howes podcast	29th Aug 2016
Einstein, Albert	In a letter to his son Eduard- from 2007 Walter Isaacson biography, "Einstein his life and universe."	5th Feb 1930
Einstein, Albert	Paraphrased "Samples, 1976" which is apparently The Metaphoric Mind by Bob Samples (which also seems to be the earliest published variant)… two sections that attribute it to Einstein, but as a paraphrase rather than a direct quote. (the intuitive mind quote)	1976
Einstein, Albert	Misattributed: Saw this in an infographic. It's all over the web, but I haven't seen it attested anywhere. https://en.wikiquote.org/wiki/Talk:Albert_Einstein#You_never_fail_until_you_stop_trying (if you've never failed quote)	1879- 1955
Einstein, Albert	Misattributed: Article by Aesop Jr (everybody is a genius quote)	1898
Eliot, T S	Little Gidding	Sept 1942
Ellington, Duke	Duke: A life of Duke Ellington	2013
Epstein, Donny	Master your energy and heal your body with Lewis Howes podcast	22nd Mar 2018
Erkic, Ana	Being Mentally Strong Is About How You Recharge, Not How You Endure. https://www.lifehack.org/521684/being-mentally-strong-is-about-how-yourecharge-not-how-you-endure	2017
Fargo, Tim	Tim Fargo on Alphabet success, The mass amplify show with Britt Michaelian	Nov 2014
Ferris, Tim	Become superhuman at any skill with Lewis Howes podcast.	29th Apr 2015
	How to overcome fear, practice self love and build a writing routine with Marie Forleo podcast.	28th Nov 2017
Fields, Jonathan	Overcoming challenge and building a champion life interviewing Lewis Howes by GoodLifeProject.	22nd May 2013
	How to live a good life with Lewis Howes podcast.	17th Oct 2016.
Fitt, Mark	The truth about success in the business of fitness with Lewis Howes.	11th Jan 2017
Fletcher, Emily	How to listen to your inner voice MindValley podcast with Vishen Lakhiani	21st Aug 2016
Forleo, Marie	MarieTV www.marieforleo.com interviews with Tony Robbins, Elizabeth Gilbert, Cathy Collaut, Seth Goddin, Simon Sinek, Renee Mauborgne, Todd Herman, Mark Manson and many more	Marie TV since 2011

Frankl, Viktor	Man's search for meaning	1946
Fuller, Margaret	The complete works of Margaret Fuller: women in the nineteenth century	19th Mar 2018
Fuller, Thomas	A Pisgah-Sight Of Palestine And The Confines Thereof, religious travelogue, contains this view	1650
Gates, Bill	At Live8 reported by BBC News	2nd July 2005
Gawdat, Mo	Solve for happy: engineer your path to joy, talks at Google.	24th Mar 2017
	The happiness equation with Lewis Howes podcast	4th Apr 2017
George, Bill	Discover your true north talks at Google. Harvard business review	2nd Nov 2015
George, Sims, McLean and Mayer	Discovering your authentic leadership	2nd Feb 2007
Gilbert, Elizabeth	Success failure and the drive to keep creating, Ted Talk.	25th Apr 2014
	Elizabeth Gilbert at Oprah's life you want tour.	17th Sept 2014
	Fear authenticity and big magic, Marie Forleo podcast.	22nd Sept 2015
	Creating big magic with Lewis Howes podcast.	13th June 2016
Gingrich, Newt	Renewing American Civilization, Class 2, speaker of the house, republican revolution	1979-1999
Glaser, Judith E.	Conversational intelligence: how great leaders build trust and get extraordinary results	2013
Glassman, Greg	The future of fitness with Lewis Howes Podcast	27th Nov 2016
Godin, Seth	Seth Godin on marketing, storytelling, attention and the future of work, Nordic business forum.	29th Aug 2016
	How to be a Linchpin, Seth Goddin on Impact Theory podcast	13th Mar 2018
Goldsmith, Marshall	Marshall Goldsmith talks at Google.	10th Dec 2007
	Triggers: creating behaviour that lasts becoming the person you want to be.	3rd Mar 2015
	A Conversation with Marshall Goldsmith and Sam Shriver podcast: 5 ways to become a better leader as defined by my mentor Dr Paul Hersey of Situational leadership model	16th Nov 2016
Gordon, Shep	Rockstars fame and celebrities: what really matters with Lewis Howes, podcast.	19 Sept 2016.
Graham Bell, Alexander	Misattributed: Was actually Helen Keller, "We bereaved"	1929

Graziosi, Dean	Millionaire success habits with Lewis Howes podcast	4th Jan 2017
Greene, Robert	Master the laws of human nature. Podcast with Robert Green, Lewis Howes	31st Oct 2018
Greenspan, Alan	As quoted in the Financial Times, An interview with Alan Greenspan, by Gillian Tett	Oct 25th, 2013,
Greiner, Sybille	On her facebook post 9th October 2017	9th Oct 2017
Hawthorne, Nathaniel	Misattributed: In June 1848 a newspaper called "The Daily Crescent" in New Orleans, Louisiana printed a set of sixteen definitions for terms such as "Love", "Faith", "Truth", "Wealth", and "Experience". The article was labelled "For the Crescent", so this article may have been the original publication. The author was only identified by the single initial "L". The butterfly metaphor was presented within the definition for "Happiness"—A butterfly, which when pursued, seems always just beyond your grasp; but if you sit down quietly, may alight upon you.	June 1848
Herman, Tod	5 steps to change your life and make it stick with Marie Forleo podcast	29th Apr 2014
Hicks, Abraham	You will get it when you can feel it, manifest in one day, copyrighted by Esther Hicks	15th Sept 2017
Hof, Wim	Mastering your breath, body and mind with Lewis Howes	26th Oct 2016
Holiday, Ryan	Overcoming your ego, podcast with Lewis Howes	11th July 2016
	The keys to a good life, podcast with Tom Bilyeu.	16th Jan 2018
	Speed isn't the key to success, podcast with Marie Forleo.	1st May 2018
Howes, Lewis	The School of Greatness podcasts.	Jan 2013 to present
	The Mask of Masculinity book.	31st Oct 2017
Huffman, Ashley	5 ways to get out of a funk. https://www.lifehack.org/433503/5-ways-to-get-out-of-a-funk	7th Mar 2017
James, William	The will to believe	1896
Jeffers, Susan	Feel the fear and do it anyway. 5 Truths in Chapter 2	2005
Johnson, Lucy	CEO Fullybookedformula.com, speaking at a Conference	March 2017
Jordan, Michael	I can't accept not trying: Michael Jordan on the pursuit of excellence Harper San Francisco p129	1994
Jung, Carl	The Phenomenology of the Self . Collected Works of C.G. Jung", Princeton University Press. 1951 Princeton university press. Retrieved 1st January 2014	1st Jan 2014

Kaizen method	Definition taken from - valuebasedmanagement.net . Masaaki Imai (born, 1930) is a Japanese organizational theorist and management consultant, known for his work on quality management, specifically on Kaizen. In 1985 he founded the Kaizen Institute Consulting Group (KICG) to help western companies introduce the concepts, systems and tools of Kaizen	1985
Keller, Helen	The story of my life	1903
Kimsey-House, Henry and Karen	Co-active Coaching Co-active Leadership	15th Dec 2010 21st Sept 2015
Klaff, Oren	Pitch anything, London Real podcast	22nd June 2014
Knost, L R	Whispers through time: communication through the ages	June 2013
Kotler, Steve	Hack your brain and new technology to reach peak performance with Lewis Howes podcast.	20th Feb 2017
Krishnaji	The power of creating a spiritual vision with Lewis Howes podcast	12th Dec 2016
La Porte, Danielle	How to visualise results and actually get things done with Marie Forleo podcast. The fire starter sessions a soulful and practical guide to creating success on your own terms. Own your truth with Lewis Howes podcast	16th Apr 2012 17th Apr 2012 8th May 2017.
Laurie, Hugh	Full post from Hugh Laurie's facebook: "It's a terrible thing, I think, in life to wait until you're ready. I have this feeling now that actually no one is ever ready to do anything. There's almost no such thing as ready. There's only now. And you may as well do it now. I mean, I say that confidently as if I'm about to go bungee jumping or something - I'm not. I'm not a crazed risk taker. But I do think that, generally speaking, now is as good a time as any."	30th Mar 2014
Law of Attraction	In the New Thought philosophy, the Law of Attraction is the belief that by focusing on positive or negative thoughts, people can bring positive or negative experiences into their life. The New Thought movement (also Higher Thought) is a movement which developed in the United States in the 19th century, considered by many to have been derived from the unpublished writings of Phineas Quimby	19th century
Lawrence, Iskra	Ending the pursuit of perfection TEDx talks University of Nevada	6th Feb 2017
Lee, Bruce	Bruce Lee: Words from a master	1st Dec 1998
Lee, Jon	The Startup article medium.com, How fear of embarrassment turned into a $12.3 billion valuation	23rd July 2018

Lencioni, Patrick	The four traits of healthy teams with Prof Marta Elvira IESE business school	24th Nov 2011
Levine, Steven	A year to live: how to live this year as if it were your last	1997
Lynch, David	Catching the big fish: meditation, consciousness and creativity	28th Dec 2006
Macdonald, George	The Marquis of Lossie	1877
Mandino, Og	The greatest salesman in the world	1968
Manson, Mark	How to stop caring about things that don't matter, Maria Forleo podcast.	16th May 2017
	Dream less do more and create real happiness with Lewis Howes podcast	16th Aug 2017
Mantell, Michael R	Don't sweat the small stuff, PS it's all small stuff.	Sept 1988
Marcinko, Richard	Rogue Warrior	1992
Maslow, Abraham	The psychology of science	1966 p15
Mattone, John	What I learned coaching Steve Jobs, seminar, World business and executive coach summit 2017	1st June 2017
Maxwell, John C	The 5 levels of leadership lunch and learn	4th Oct 2011
Mckay, Dr Sarah	Outrospection term used: http://yourbrainhealth.com.au/this-is-your-brain-onempathy/	21st Aug 2016
Milton, John	Paradise Lost, Book I	1667
Misner, Dr Ivan	Success: The Uncommon Application of Common Knowledge podcast	12th June 2012
Myss, Caroline	The Caroline Myss and Wayne Dyer Seminar	May 2003
Ngo, Kevin	Let's Do This! 100 Powerful Messages to Help You Take Action	26th Sept 2013
Nichols, Lisa	Abundance now: amplify your life and achieve prosperity today	2016 Harper
Orman. Suze	The courage to be rich	1999
Orr, David	David Orr's book Ecological Literacy: Educating Our Children for a Sustainable World	25th Oct 2005

Pay Hinckley, Marjorie	Small and Simple Things	2003
Peters, Prof Steve	The Chimp Paradox: The Mind Management Programme to Help You Achieve Success, Confidence and Happiness Paperback	5th Jan 2012
Pink, Daniel H	Drive: the surprising truth about what motivates us	29th Dec 2009
Plato	This was Plato's account of Socrates. It is also called the Socratic paradox. The phrase is not one that Socrates himself is ever recorded as saying	1509-1511
Porchon-Lynch, Tao	Her facebook entry. Don't let age dictate what you can and cannot do. Tao Porchon-Lynch 97-year-old yoga teacher	15th Oct 2016
Pressfield, Steven	4 questions to help you find your calling, Supersoul Oprah podcast	29th Sept 2013
Raveling, George	Coach George Raveling interview in the Tim Ferriss Show Podcast	21st Sept 2018
Rees, Jim	The long and short of it presentation at CIPD meeting	June 2017
Robbins, Mel	How to stop screwing yourself over, TEDxSF. Why motivation is garbage, Impact theory podcast. The 5 second rule to change your life with Lewis Howes podcast. How to beat self doubt in 5 seconds success talks podcast	11th June 2011 31st Jan 2017 1st Mar 2017 2nd Nov 2017.
Robbins, Tony	Awaken the giant within. Why we do what we do, TED conference. Relationship breakthrough, Madanes and Robbins. Personal strategy, National achievers congress. Money master the game. https://www.tonyrobbins.com/leadership-impact/thesecret-to-living-is-giving/ (secret to living quote) What it takes to have an extraordinary life interview with Marie Forleo podcast Giant Steps	1991 16th Jan 2007 23rd Sept 2012 18th Nov 2014 27th Aug 2015 26th Jan 2016 19th July 2016 14th June 2017
Robinson, Ken	Do schools kill creativity, TED talks	6 Jan 2007
Rock, David	SCARF model developed in his paper "SCARF: A Brain-Based Model for Collaborating With and Influencing Others."	2008
Rohn, Jim	Jim Rohn: Stop wasting any more time speech on youtube, source www.jimrohn.com	10th June 2018

Author	Title	Date
Roosevelt, Teddy	Address at the prize day exercises at Groton School,	24th May 1904
Rowe, Mike	What 300 dirty jobs taught him about true success with Lewis Howes podcast	7th Nov 2016
Ruez, Don Miguel	The Four Agreements: A Practical Guide to Personal Freedom	Nov 1997
Rumi	The essential Rumi	1273
Sawubona	Zulu greeting Zulu kingdom	Established 1816
Schwarzenegger, Arnold	Arnold Schwarzenegger's motivation 6 rules of success speech	28th Dec 2012
Shapiro, Dani	Writing process and the myth of inspiration with Marie Forleo podcast	23rd Jan 2018
Sharma, Robin S	The monk who sold his ferrari	1996
Shetty, Jay	Cultivate a monk mindset with Jay Shetty and Lewis Howes podcast	27th Feb 2018
Sinek, Simon	If you don't understand people you don't understand business, 99U podcast.	16th Nov 2012
	Why leaders eat last 99U podcast.	4th Dec 2013
	How to be a great leader inspiring others to do remarkable things, Marie Forleo podcast.	7th June 2016
	Simon Sinek on how to get people to follow you, Inside quest.	28th Oct 2016
	Simon Sinek's Top 10 rules for success Evan Carmichael podcast.	14th Nov 2016
	The Finite and Infinite games of leadership, talks at Google.	19th June 2017
	Undersranding empathy, Justin McClung podcast.	2nd Aug 2017
Singh, Lilly	5 things you do that make you unhappy youtube superwoman podcast.	17th July 2015
	How to turn depression into millions on Impact theory podcast.	7th Aug 2018
Smith, Julia	Human Emotions Vibration Analysis Frequency Ranges. https://thesevenminds.wordpress.com/2014/04/08/emotional-energy/	2012
Soloman, King	Proverbs of Soloman 17:22	700 BC
St Thomas	The Gospel of Thomas	40AD- 140AD
Strayed, Cheryl	Radical sincerity TEDx Concordia.	22nd Apr 2012
	Love life and lessons learned in the wild Concordia University.	3rd Nov 2014
	Reese Witherspoon Laura Dern and Cheryl Strayed Wild interview.	6th Dec 2014
	Don't let your dreams ruin your life, Oprah Supersoul sessions.	6th June 2016

	How to become a writer, The power of art and more Marie Forleo podcast.	21st Feb 2017.
Thompson, Hunter S	Letter to his friend Hume Logan	July 1957
Tillich, Paul	The courage to be	1952
Tolle, Eckhart	How do we break the habit of excessive thinking podcast?	3rd Oct 2011
	How to silence voices in your head, Supersoul podcast.	11th Nov 2012
	Conversations on compassion podcast.	21st Feb 2013
	The importance of being extraordinary -goals podcast.	22nd Aug 2013
	Settling into presence podcast.	23rd Oct 2014
	Waiting with presence podcast.	8th Feb 2016
	Laughter breaks through the ego, podcast.	8th Mar 2016
	Eckhart Tolle's advice that Oprah says eliminated all stress in her life, Supersoul podcast.	22nd Oct 2017
	Free yourself from anxiety Supersoul podcast.	23rd Oct 2017
Valderrama, Wilmer	Create fearless confidence and achieve anything with Lewis Howes podcast	23rd July 2017
Van Edwards, Vanessa	The science of people with Lewis Howes podcast.	23rd Apr 2017
	You are contagious, TEDx London	27th June 2017
Velzeboer, Petra	In my conversations with Petra Velzeboer. Speaker, Coach, Mental health consultant	19th March 2017
Vobora, David	The power of pain to transform into your best self with Lewis Howes podcast	30th May 2017
Whitworth, Laura	Co-Active Coaching	1998
Williamson, Marianne	A Return to Love: Reflections on the Principles of A Course in Miracles is the first book by author Marianne Williamson and a New York Times Best seller.	Harper Collins1992
Woodward, Sir Clive	The DNA of a champion, Sir Clive Woodward interviewed by Piers Morgan, Louise Hunter podcast at minute 29	24th June 2016

Pictures - photographer list

Front cover - Colin Behrens - lightbulb - Bielefeld Germany

Umbrellas - Gerd Altman, Freiburg Germany

Target - Skeeze, USA

Team sports - Skeeze, USA

Team sports - Paul Want, Natland England

Lonely - Siska, Jakarta Indonesia

Team sports - Pexels, England

Team sports - Quim Muns, Sant Cugat del Valles Spain

Sports - Scott Webb, London and Canada

Leadership - Tumisu, England

Fight - Mario Hofer, Steyregg Austria

Rules - Lockie, England

Achieve - Free photos, England

Sunrise - Sasin Tipchai, Amphoe Phochai Thailand

Glass - Public domain pictures England

Mystical - Free photos, England

Riding bicycle - Mabel Amber, England

City lights - photographer ID 12019

Blue planet - Orlando, Heidelberg Germany

Mystical - Jonny Lindner, Germany

Sad - Ryan McGuire, Ithaca New York

Sad - Lisa Runnels, Magee USA

Glass - Jonas Svidras, Vilnius Lithuania

Finger print - Foundry company, Dallas USA

Peace - Sasin Tipchai, Amphoe Phochai Thailand

Lion - Ian Lindsay, South Africa

Love - Skeeze, USA

Hidden - SplitShire, England

Team sports - Lovemybry, England

Artist - Alexandr Ivanov, Yaroslavl Russia

Artist - Pexels, England

Mystical - Stefan Keller, Germany

Compass - Dima Goroziya, Russia

Courage - Jonny Lindner, Germany

Sad - Wilhan Jose Gomes, Londrina Brazil

High heels - Marlene Bitzer, Tubingen Germany

Jump - Skeeze, USA

Sad - Ryan McGuire, Ithaca New York

Self - Andry Richardson, Buffalo USA

Sports - Jonny Lindner, Germany

Fantasy - Free-Photos, England

Run - Pexels, England

Puppy - Anastasia Geppe, Chelyabinsk Russia

Teach - Sasin Tipchai, Amphoe Phochai Thailand

Stars - Free-Photos, England

Sports - Sasin Tipchai, Amphoe Phochai Thailand

Love - Silvia and Frank, Germany

Signpost - Jan Alexander, Fort Collins USA

Intelligent - WikiImages, Germany

Teach - Gerd Altman, Freiburg Germany

Climbing tree - Skeeze, USA

Hug - StockSnap, England

Opposites - Gerd Altman, Freiburg Germany

Scary - Public Domain Pictures, England

Chakra - Karin Henseler, Koln Bonn Germany

Helping - Patrick Neufelder, Schluchsee Germany

Rescue - Skeeze, USA

Team work - Rawpixel, England

Action - Web Donut, Belgrade Serbia

Laugh - Silvia/Silviarita, Germany

Self - Svklimkin, Moscow Russia

Hole - FreePhotos, England

Training - ID 5132824

Success - Nattanan Kanchanaprat, Bangkok Thailand

Dive - FreePhotos, England

Map - Lorri Lang, England

Self - Gerd Altman, Freiburg Germany

About the Author

Rachael Orchard has produced the PASSION Toolset as part of a simple to use system for Initiative Fatigue for coaches, leaders and students of learning. It sets forth a new methodology that quickly identifies mental blocks to learning or goals completion. It can be used as part of personal development, your own online learning, or through a work or educational community.

Rachael started running small businesses in events and marketing, but very quickly realised how much she cared about people and the best place to influence people was in their personal development.

After years of coaching many hundreds of people individually and in teams it became apparent that enabling people to shift their mental blocks by focusing on small daily behavioural tasks was transformative and something that really works.

For the last couple of years Rachael has been developing this theory, which culminated in extensive market testing last year and during the test period had coaches crying out for a PASSION Toolset book.

When Rachael's not writing, coaching or designing what could become ground breaking courses, she can be found training as an on-call fire fighter, looking after her two beautiful children and generally doing anything adrenaline based that involves muscle cars or the Red Arrows!

Rachael lives in Cambridgeshire in the United Kingdom. She hopes that the PASSION Toolset enables you to knock your goals out of the ball park.

Rachael Orchard, Coach, Speaker, Author